Brigitte Okley Ainuson

Implementation of International environmental law and policy

Brigitte Okley Ainuson

Implementation of International environmental law and policy

A Case Study of Ghana

LAP LAMBERT Academic Publishing

Impressum/Imprint (nur für Deutschland/only for Germany)
Bibliografische Information der Deutschen Nationalbibliothek: Die Deutsche
Nationalbibliothek verzeichnet diese Publikation in der Deutschen Nationalbibliografie;
detaillierte bibliografische Daten sind im Internet über http://dnb.d-nb.de abrufbar.
Alle in diesem Buch genannten Marken und Produktnamen unterliegen warenzeichen-,
marken- oder patentrechtlichem Schutz bzw. sind Warenzeichen oder eingetragene
Warenzeichen der jeweiligen Inhaber. Die Wiedergabe von Marken, Produktnamen,
Gebrauchsnamen, Handelsnamen, Warenbezeichnungen u.s.w. in diesem Werk berechtigt
auch ohne besondere Kennzeichnung nicht zu der Annahme, dass solche Namen im Sinne
der Warenzeichen- und Markenschutzgesetzgebung als frei zu betrachten wären und
daher von jedermann benutzt werden dürften.

Coverbild: www.ingimage.com

Verlag: LAP LAMBERT Academic Publishing GmbH & Co. KG
Dudweiler Landstr. 99, 66123 Saarbrücken, Deutschland
Telefon +49 681 3720-310, Telefax +49 681 3720-3109
Email: info@lap-publishing.com

Approved by: University of Georgia, Athens, Diss 2004

Herstellung in Deutschland:
Schaltungsdienst Lange o.H.G., Berlin
Books on Demand GmbH, Norderstedt
Reha GmbH, Saarbrücken
Amazon Distribution GmbH, Leipzig
ISBN: 978-3-8454-0512-4

Imprint (only for USA, GB)
Bibliographic information published by the Deutsche Nationalbibliothek: The Deutsche
Nationalbibliothek lists this publication in the Deutsche Nationalbibliografie; detailed
bibliographic data are available in the Internet at http://dnb.d-nb.de.
Any brand names and product names mentioned in this book are subject to trademark,
brand or patent protection and are trademarks or registered trademarks of their respective
holders. The use of brand names, product names, common names, trade names, product
descriptions etc. even without a particular marking in this works is in no way to be
construed to mean that such names may be regarded as unrestricted in respect of
trademark and brand protection legislation and could thus be used by anyone.

Cover image: www.ingimage.com

Publisher: LAP LAMBERT Academic Publishing GmbH & Co. KG
Dudweiler Landstr. 99, 66123 Saarbrücken, Germany
Phone +49 681 3720-310, Fax +49 681 3720-3109
Email: info@lap-publishing.com

Printed in the U.S.A.
Printed in the U.K. by (see last page)
ISBN: 978-3-8454-0512-4

Copyright © 2011 by the author and LAP LAMBERT Academic Publishing GmbH & Co. KG
and licensors
All rights reserved. Saarbrücken 2011

LEGISLATION AND IMPLEMENTATION OF INTERNATIONAL ENVIRONMENTAL LAW BY AFRICAN COUNTRIES: A CASE STUDY OF GHANA

By

BRIGITTE LISA MAMLE OKLEY

DEDICATION

This work is dedicated to the Glory of God Almighty, who strengthens me to do all things.

ACKNOWLEDGEMENTS

I would like to thank Professor Bodansky and Professor Wilner for their guidance and encouragement during the course of this research.

My sincere thanks to my family, Kweku Ainuson and Florence Addo for their love, support and encouragement; you have helped me reach this far.

TABLE OF CONTENTS

Page

ACKNOWLEDGMENTS..v

CHAPTER

1. INTRODUCTION..1
   A. International Environmental Law...1
   B. State of the environment in Ghana..3
2. IMPLEMENTATION..7
   A. Implementation of International Environmental Agreements..............7
   B. Factors that Influences Implementation................................8
   C. Other Aspects of Implementation.......................................12
3. INTERNATIONAL ENVIRONMENTAL AGREEMENTS AND NATIONAL IMPLEMENTATION..14
   A. Effect of International Environmental Agreements in Ghana............14
   B. Institutional Framework...16
   C. Environmental Legislation in Ghana....................................24
   D. Environmental Impact Assessment.......................................48
4. OBSTACLES TO IMPLEMENTATION IN GHANA..........................56
5. RECOMMENDATION..62
6. CONCLUSION..69
7. BIBLIOGRAPHY..71

CHAPTER I: INTRODUCTION

A. International Environmental Law

International Environmental Law emerged in the latter part of the 20th century as a distinctive branch of International law. It emerged as a response to the heightened awareness of the degradation of our human environment. Growing danger to the environment due to over population, destructive human activities, industry and technology led to the realization that the natural order and human wellbeing was at a serious risk and that a global and regional (depending on the nature of the problem) effort was required to address the issue. For issues like acid rain it was a regional problem and for others like climate change it was global. In response to this, the UN organized the Stockholm Conference on Human Environment[1] in 1972 after years of study and discussions on global basis. After ten years and in commemoration of the tenth anniversary of the Stockholm Conference, the United Nations Conference on Environment and Development[2] 1992 known as the Rio conference was also organized. Following these conferences, the international community in their quest to protect and conserve the environment and its immense species has entered into numerous Multilateral Environmental Agreements. African countries also in their efforts to promote environmental quality have adopted many Multilateral Environmental Agreements under the aegis of the OAU. Major regional agreements entered into by African countries including Ghana seeks to reinforce global agreements by filling in gaps, facilitating joint

---

[1] See United Nations Conference on Human Environment, June 16, 1972, 11 I.L.M. 1416 (1972)
[2] See Rio Declaration on Environment and Development, June, 1992, 31I.L.M. 874

action and mutual understanding in environmental policy and management, and enabling environmental issues to be treated on a regional rather than national basis.

Ghana, like most African countries, harbors immense biodiversity. African countries like Ghana depend a lot on these biodiversities than any other continent in the world. This is the basis for agriculture, which is the main economic activity in most part of rural areas. It is estimated that agriculture provides employment for 75% of the country's rural population. Export of agriculture products, timber and eco-tourism forms a substantial part of the foreign exchange earning in Ghana. Poverty is a major cause and consequence of environmental degradation and resource depletion in Ghana. Major environmental problems include deforestation, desertification, and soil degradation, water scarcity, decline in biodiversity and marine resources and marine pollution. These problems are due to poor agricultural practices, urbanization, debt problems and inadequate environmental policies.

Before the Stockholm Conference, Ghana dealt with environmental problems on ad-hoc basis, which was very limited in scope. Ghana enacted many laws that empowered various bodies to manage certain aspect of the environment. After the Stockholm Conference in 1972, Ghana created an environmental policy institution-the Environmental Protection Council[3], which performed among other things research, advisory roles, and coordinated activities of other bodies concerned with resource and environmental management. Subsequent to the Rio Conference[4] Ghana redefined its environmental policy to achieve sustainable development.

---

[3] See Environmental Protection Decree of Ghana 1974 [hereinafter EPC] (note, the members of the EPC were from the ministries of Health, Foreign Affairs, Land and Natural Resources, Agriculture, Local Government, Finance, Economic Planning, Science and technology and Works and Housing.
[4] Also known as the United Nation Conference on Environment and Development (UNCED) 1992

This paper focuses on Ghana because the author is familiar with Environmental policy in Ghana. The main purpose of this paper is to briefly examine how effective Ghana has implemented it environmental commitments under international law. The first part of the paper examines the state of the environment in Ghana. The second part of the paper will examine implementation of Multilateral Environmental Agreements generally by looking at some of the factors that influence implementation, and approaches and theories of implementation. The third part examines typical Multilateral Environmental Agreements Ghana has ratified that addresses its environmental problems and how it has adopted policies to implement them. Finally, the paper will examine some of the obstacles to implementation in Ghana and suggest recommendations for overcoming the obstacles.

B. State of the Environment in Ghana

Ghana covers an area of 239,460 square kilometers and is situated in the Central Southern part of West Africa along the Gulf of Guinea.[5] It extends between 4.5 degrees north on its southern coast and extends 11 degrees north into the inland. This makes its location very near to the equator. It is bordered on the north by Burkina Faso, on the east by Togo, on the west by Cote-d'Ivoire and on the south by the Gulf of Guinea. It spans two major ecological zones; the savannah woodlands which covers the north and coastal areas and the high forest zone, centered in the southwestern part of the country.[6] The environmental situation in Ghana is almost the same as many other African states. This is characterized by acute shortage of water in the north, soil erosion, desertification, soil

---

[5] *Available at: Http:// www.ghana.gov.gh/governing/ministries/social/environment.php*

[6] *See Fact file of Ghana; available at: http:// www.actionaid.org/resources/pdfs/ghana*

degradation and deforestation. High population growth rate, estimated at 3% per annum[7], urbanization due to rural out-migration, poverty and increasing debt servicing have intensified the environmental problems. The state of the environment in Ghana is currently not in the best of shapes.

1. **Land and Food**

The agricultural sector is the backbone of Ghana's economy employing about 75% of the total population[8] and accounts for more than 40% of the GNP. The outmoded practice of clearing forest by bushfires before cultivation has led to a decline in agricultural yields over the years thereby putting pressure on land for cultivation. This is also a major cause of desertification.

2. **Biological Diversity**: *In Ghana about 2,974 indigenous plant, 450 fish, 728 bird, 225 Mammal, 221 amphibian and reptile species have so far been recorded.*[9] *The depletion of Ghana's biodiversity is alarming. The decline is a result of indiscriminate killing for consumption and sale on the international market.*

3. **Deforestation:** *The Environmental Protection Council (EPC)* [10] *reported that more than 90% of the original 8.22 million hectares of natural forest woodland in Ghana has been logged since the 1940s mainly for timber export, fuel wood for domestic and industrial use and agricultural land clearing. In arid and semi-arid areas, one of the serious consequences of deforestation is desertification. It is estimated that 35% of the total land is subject to desertification. Many of Ghana's forest reserves which were*

---

[7] *Supra* note 5; Ghana's population is now estimated to be 20.2 million
[8] See EPC. Rep. VOL. 1 (1991)
[9] At: http://allafrica.com/stories/200305220076.html
[10] See Ghana's Environmental Action Plan. Vol. 1 (EPC 1991) [hereinafter Environmental Action Plan]

created as shelterbelts against the savannah winds and as protection for headwaters have been lost, due to excessive logging and bushfires.

4. **Marine Resources and Coastal Zones**

Ghana's marine resources and costal zones are under threat from over-fishing, urbanization and development related activities. Increased fishing as a result of growing demand for protein and employment coupled with advanced fishing technologies and growing number of commercial vessels have led to over-exploitation of fishes. The problem of over-exploitation has been made worse by the expansion of the jurisdiction of coastal states to 200 miles under the Exclusive Economic Zone regime of United Nations Convention on the Law of the Sea. The expanded coastline has now been left at the mercy of long distance fishing fleets shipping on commercial basis because Ghana lacks the requisite resources for effective policing. The population along the coastal areas represents 25% of the total population of Ghana. Apart from housing individuals and their families, it also houses the major industrial companies, as a result, discharges, household refuse, oil waste, chemicals and other material pollutes the coastal zones. Shipping, dredging and drilling for oil and gas off the west coast also causes pollution. Oil pollution is a chronic problem, it is estimated that 5%of oil spills in Ghana have resulted from tanker accidents and 95% from terminal operations[11]. Thus, oil pollution along the coast is a major cause for alarm. Consequently, 12 of Ghana's 16 coastal lagoons are heavily polluted. The Korle lagoon is an example of such polluted lagoons. Beaches are soiled with untreated household waste and erosion along the coastal communities has resulted in loss of houses to the coastal communities. More than 90%

---

[11] See Emmanuel K. Boon, Legal and Economic Environmental Policy in Ghana VUB Brussels, Belgium also available at: http:// www.vub.ac.be/MEKO/publications/epghana.doc

of the buildings in Keta (which is in the Volta Region of Ghana) have been lost to erosion. Studies conducted with the assistance of the Norwegian Government[12] have shown that illegal activities and the use of deadly chemicals in fishing have significantly depleted the deep-sea stock.

These are but a list of some of the environmental issues in Ghana. There are other environmental concerns like urbanization, water quality, and pollution from mining, environmental refugees and displacement. The pictured depicted above indicates an environment stressed by desertification, deforestation, and land degradation through unorthodox agricultural practices. Inadequate environmental laws and policy further impounds the problem as will soon be apparent.

---

[12] *See Sarah Simpson, Fishing for a Future, BBC Mar. 19,2003 available at http://www.globalpolicy.org/socecon/develop/2003/0319fishfuture.htm*

CHAPTER II: IMPLEMENTATION

A. Implementation of International Environmental Agreements

Implementation here refers to national measures and policy responses that countries adopt to put into action international obligations. Some international agreements are self-executing, meaning they do not require domestic legislation to become effective. However, most Multilateral Environmental Agreements require states to enact legislations and regulations to implement them.

Even though a state may enact legislation to implement international obligations, this is not the same as complying with the provisions of the agreement. Thus, compliance refers to whether a contracting party or a state has strictly adhered to the provisions of the particular agreements it purports to implement. Compliance involves the question; to what extent has the state followed through the guidelines and provisions of the agreement to implement it? Assessing whether there has been compliance is a matter of judgment. The ultimate aim of Multilateral Environmental Agreements is to cause a change in or influence the behavior of those who cause or can ameliorate the environmental problem at hand. This is the point at which one can say that implementation has been effective. Even though implementation may be effective, it does not totally eliminate the environmental problem at hand, rather it is the means by which objectives of an environmental agreement is achieved. On the other hand, a country may comply with an agreement, but such compliance may be ineffective in attaining the objectives of the agreement. One author illustrate this point by noting that, "compliance with an international agreement may result in the cessation of an activity that contributed to the pollution, but might lead to an overall increase of pollution by encouraging other activities the consequences of which were equally bad or even worse."[13] Implementing obligations is one thing and achieving effectiveness is another. Many factors contribute to effective implementation of obligations and effectiveness of international environmental agreement. These factors would work depending on the specific circumstances of each state.

B. Factors That Influences Implementation

Many factors essential in influencing effective implementation have been identified. These factors according to some authors are not exhaustive and it is very difficult to say precisely which is the most important.[14] Some of these factors have been identified as follows: nature of the problem, nature of the accord, circumstances of the country, and configuration of powers

1. Nature of the Problem

Studies have confirmed that the smaller the number of actors involved in causing environmental problem the easier it is to effectively regulate such an activity. Thus, some problems are easier to address and regulate than other, hence some international agreement will be easier to implement than others will. The reason being that not only is it easier, but also less expensive, and it affects the cost-benefit ratio, the distribution of those costs, benefits, and the economic competitiveness. Therefore, where some problems can be resolved at a low cost, implementation is effective. For example, because a limited number of facilities produced ozone depleting substances through the

---

[13] See Mats Rolen et al., International Governance on Environmental Issues 83 (1997).
[14] See David Victor et al., Implementation and Effectiveness of International Environmental Commitments: Theory and Practice 15-18 (1998).

early 1990s, it was relatively very easy to control the emissions of those substances as was required by the Montreal Protocol[15] and its amendments. The situation could become more difficult as more production facilities come online in the latter half of the 1990s. On the other hand, when some problem exhibit high cost and targets are aware of the cost involved, benefits may be meager and diffuse. The difference between the number of facilities that produced ozone depleting substances and the millions of people who engaged in illicit trade in endangered species explains why it was very difficult to enforce Convention in International Trade in Endangered Species. This was because those engaged in illicit trading move in smaller and less visible groups, than those big multinational corporations owning facilities that produce ozone-depleting substances. These large firms are concerned about their reputation on the international arena and they can be subjected to pressure from consumers and public opinion throughout the world to produce ozone friendly products.[16]

2.   **Nature of the Accord**

The nature of the accords or commitments may have a strong influence on implementation. Studies have shown that when the obligation is precise in scope, the application it is easier for parties to access and successfully implement them.[17] In the international regime for oil pollution resulting from operations of shipping vessels, the rules on allowing discharge of oil to a required amount did not influence tanker captains

---

[15] See The Montreal Protocol on Substance that Deplete the Ozone Layer, Sept. 16, 1987, 26 I.L.M. 1550 [hereinafter Montreal Protocol].

[16] Rolen, supra note 13 at 93(where Edith Brown Weiss gave example of how the Montreal Protocol and the London Convention worked in big nations like the U.S, Brazil, EU, and India)

to comply because their behavior could not easily be monitored on the high seas hence there was no incentive to comply as it merely deterred them. The equipment standard on the other hand, were far more effective because it required ship owners to install segregated ballast tanks to limit oily discharges, these requirements were not only easy to monitor it was also very difficult not to comply with it.[18]

3. Characteristics of the Country

Countries are subject to Multilateral Environmental Agreements they are at the center of implementation and compliance process and must take steps to fulfill their obligations. It is argued that the varying circumstances of a particular country will determine how effectively it fulfills its obligations. Thus, how well a country does in implementing its obligation will depend on "what it traditionally did with respect to the issue being dealt with and the legislation and regulations that it already had in place at the time it became a party to the accord."[19] Richer and more democratic countries would generally do better in implementing their obligations than poorer and less developed countries. This variance may be looked at in terms of administrative capacity. Developed countries have effective administrative capacity due to the availability of knowledge evidence in having highly educated and trained personnel in that field. They also have strong financial backbones and relevant access to information, backed by legal mandate to be effective. Economic factors indirectly play a very important role in effective implementation. The rate of growth of a country's GNP has very little effect on implementation however

---

[17] See Ron Mitchell, "Regime Design Matters: International Oil Pollution and Treaty Compliance," 48 Int. Org. 425 (1994)
[18] Id. at 427-428
[19] Rolen, supra 13, (noting that traditional behavior is deeply embedded in a country's culture)

economic chaos or collapse can have serious implications. This is because limited government resources plus high inflationary rate will have a profound effect on the incentives of administrative agencies to enforce their obligations. The political system and institutions in place in a country will also make a difference in implementation. Bigger countries have a much more complicated duty of complying with commitments than smaller countries. Where the activities that the agreement deals with is widely dispersed, as in the CITES, different levels of political authority will have to be coordinated, and this is not an easy task. Political instability can also lead to decline in compliance in environmental agreements. This has affected many countries in Africa over a long period. As is evidence, democratic governments are more transparent in their dealing and are very responsive to public opinion, than military dictatorship. Pressure from domestic groups and public opinion are important mechanisms for promoting, implementing and complying with treaty obligations. Individual leaders also play major roles in implementation. The role played by various world leaders have helped shape implementation and compliance in many countries: Brazilian President Fernando Collor took special interest in the environment and played a major role in having Rio de Janeiro selected as the venue for UNCED, Former President Clinton's administration appears to have been more committed to environmental issues.

4. Configuration of Powers

Hegemonic states and powerful NGOs have major influence in implementation.[20] Powerful countries like the U.S in the international oil regime have used threat of

---

[20] Mitchell, supra note 64 at 428; see also Victor, supra note 61at15where he refer to this factor as configuration of powers.

sanction and unilateral actions to induce compliance and implementation from various states. U.S threat of sanctions also reduced the number of whales caught by Norway and stopped whaling in Iceland. Greenpeace has also played similar roles like the U.S, influencing implementation. By threats of boycotts of Iceland and Norwegian products in the U.S and Germany Greenpeace, has been able to ensure that their whaling programs are in conformity with the regime on Whaling. In addition, the actions of other countries in implementing their obligations can affect a country's compliance with an agreement.

These factors in influencing implementation and effectiveness interact in many ways and one factor is not more effective than the other. However, the process of implementation itself is central to determining effectiveness. Implementation through extensive regulatory measures and adequate policy responses including financial, economic institutions as well as public and NGOs participation can be very effective..

C   Other Aspects of Implementation

There are various aspects of implementation. Some scholars list System for Implementation Reviews and National Implementation as reflecting a central attribute of the implementation process. It helps to explain which commitments are most effective and it is sufficiently narrow to allow case studies that focus on specific issues amenable to change through policy.[21] System for Implementation Review (SIRs) is made up of rules and procedures by which parties and other interest groups to international accords share and exchange data, information on implementation; monitor activities, assess the adequacy of existing obligations, and deal with issues of poor implementation. Many

Multilateral Environmental Agreements contain provisions requiring parties to report on efforts on implementation and they contain procedures for reviewing these reports. These reports and reviews help assess the adequacy of commitments and ways to manage poor implementation. SIRs based on these reports helps to lower transaction cost and enhance international cooperation. It also makes it easier for NGOs to monitor and identify implementation problems and to pressure governments to fully implement their commitments.[22] SIRs are merely complimentary to national implementation, which is the main means of implementing commitments under Multilateral Environmental Agreements. National implementation of Multilateral Environmental Agreements is made through the creation of institutional and legislative framework by governments backed by financial transfers to set up administrative capacity needed to comply with commitments. National implementation is also accelerated by participation by stakeholders and actors with particular interested in the given issue. Patterns of participation are therefore a major part of national implementation process.[23]

---

[21] *Id.* at 15-26
[22] *Id.* at 47

CHAPTER III: INTERNATIONAL ENVIRONMENTAL CONVENTIONS AND NATIONAL IMPLEMENTATION

A. Effect of International Environmental Agreements in Ghana

This section will examine the effect of international law in Ghana and its relation with Treaties, it will address the institutional and legislative framework put in place to facilitate environmental policy making and legislation in Ghana.

Determination of how Ghana implements its obligation under international law requires discussions on the effect of international law in Ghana. The general principle is that international law is binding on a state[24] and a state is under obligation to give effect to it. However, states may make and apply international law through their government and their constitutional and their legal systems. The state is responsible in ensuring that its constitution and its laws enable the government to carry out its obligations under international law.[25] Consequently, a state cannot plead its own municipal law as a reason for non-compliance with international law[26]. This principle is reaffirmed in Article 13 of the Declaration of Rights and Duties of States prepared by the International Law Commission in 1949[27] which provides that "Every state has the duty to carry out in good faith its obligation arising from treaties and other sources of international law, and it may not invoke provisions in its constitution or its laws as an excuse for failure to perform this duty"[28] this is the relation of international law to municipal law. Two schools of thought are expressed when it comes to the relation of municipal law to international law. The

---

[23] *Id.*
[24] See Convention on the Law of Treaties May 23, 1969, 8 ILM 679, art 26 [hereinafter Vienna Convention]; This principle is base on the maxim "pacta sunt servanda".
[25] See Lori F. Damrosch "et al. eds. International Law 4th ed., 159 (2001)
[26] Vienna Convention, supra at art. 27
[27] See Declaration of Rights and Duties of States available at: http://www.un.org/law/ilc/texts.declar.htm

dualist or the pluralist regards international law and municipal law as separate legal system, which operate on different levels. For the dualist, international law can only be applied by the state courts when it has been made part of the domestic legislation through the process of either "transformation" or "incorporation". In addition, the international law as incorporated into the municipal law is subject to the constitution as other municipal laws. Monist on the other hand, regards international law and municipal law as part of a single legal system. Monist, in its traditional version, sees municipal law as deriving validity from international law, which stand high in a hierarchy of legal norms. In this case, international law is not subject to domestic laws neither is it subject to constitutional limitations.[29]

Ghana has a common law system and therefore, follows the English dualist concept. Consequently, Ghanaian courts will apply customary international law by virtue of incorporation and as long as it is consistent with an Act of Parliament. A Treaty however, has to be transformed or enacted into legislation before it can have effect and the courts can only enforce it when it has been enacted into legislation. Therefore, for Multilateral Environmental Agreements to have effect in Ghana they have to be enacted into legislation by an Act of Parliament, failing that, the treaty will only be binding on Ghana in terms of its relationship with the international community.[30] Consequently, implementation of Multilateral Environmental Agreements requires appropriate institutional and legislative framework to give them the force of law.

---

[28] Id. art. 46; see also the Chorzow factory case (Merits) P.C.I.J., Ser. A, No. 17 at 33-34 [29] Damrosch supra note 25 at 160
[30] See George Sarpong, Domestication of Biodiversity Conservation Instruments in Ghana: a UNEP/EPA Ghana Consultancy Report July 2000 (unpublished paper)

B. **Institutional Framework**

A National Environmental Policy for Ghana as defined seeks among other things to create a balance between economic development and sustainable use of its natural resources placing environmental quality high on the list of elements supporting the country's economic growth. This is in line with Principle 4 of Rio Declaration[31], which provides that to achieve sustainable development, environmental protection should constitute an integral part of the development process and not considered in isolation.

The main features of Ghana's environmental policy inter alia include developing and adopting sectoral plans; enacting legislations and regulations to give effect to Ghana's commitments under the various Multilateral Environmental Agreements it has acceded to; adopting standards and strengthening existing institutions and community groups. This is in line with Agenda 21 of Rio[32], which contain strategies and measures that states can adopt to implement sustainable and responsible development of the planet. Most prominent among them is the Environmental Protection Agency (EPA), the Ministry of Science and Environment, the District Assemblies (DA) and National Development and Planning Commission (NDPC). These institutions are assisted by various sub-institutions in the performance of their functions to ensure effective coordination and control. The main policy objectives of these institutions are to ensure sound management of Ghana's natural resources and environment, and to maintain the ecosystem and ecological processes essential for the functioning of the biosphere.

---

[31] Rio Declaration, supra note 2
[32] Id.

eliminate pollution; integrating environmental considerations into sectoral structure and socio-economic development and seeking common solutions to environmental problems in West Africa, Africa and the world at large.[33] *These objectives cover Ghana's commitments under various Multilateral Environmental Agreements it has ratified.*

Ghana has a National Environment Action Plan (NEAP), adopted by the government in 1991, and implemented since 1993 under a project called the Ghana Environmental Resource Management Project (GERMP). The Environmental Protection Agency is coordinating implementation. The NEAP addresses almost all the issues covered in Agenda 21 except the following: Sustainable Development of Small Islands; Environmentally Sound Management of Biotechnology; Safe and Environmentally Sound Management of Radioactive Wastes; and Combating Poverty. Working groups were established and they reviewed existing policies and programs related to development and environment and made recommendations for implementation in Land Management; Forestry and Wildlife; Water Management; Marine and Coastal Ecosystems; Mining, Manufacturing Industries and Hazardous Chemicals; and other areas.[34] *Other objectives include protecting flora and fauna and their habitats from intrusive and destructive practices; preserving biodiversity; directing development in such a way to reduce or if possible*

---

[33] See Environmental Protection Agency at a Glance, 1996, (unpublished report)
[34] Ministry of Environment Science and Technology, National Consultation on Implementation of the Rio Agreements and Agenda 21 in Ghana Report of Consultations Organized at Accra, January 9-10, 1997

1. **The Ministry of Science and Environment** [35]

The Ministry of science and environment replaced the Ministry of environment science and technology, established in 1993 to coordinate the implementation of Agenda 21 of Rio. It set up a National Advisory Committee for the Implementation of Agenda 21(NACIA 21), which worked closely with other government ministries and departments including the ministries of mines and energy, tourism, local government and rural development, and lands and forestry. The NACIA 21 has the mandate for policy formulation, advice and coordination. The ministry of science and environment chairs it. The Ministry of science and environment mission statement is "to establish a strong national scientific and technological base for accelerated sustainable development of the country to enhance the quality of life for all" and this is to be achieved through "the development and promotion of cost effective use of appropriate technologies, safe and sound environmental practices and efficient human settlement".[36] *The Ministry performs the following functions:*

- *Protection of the environment through formulating of policies, scientific, economic and technological interventions needed to mitigate any harmful impact caused by development related activities;*
- *Submitting proposals for legislation on the environment based on studies and consultations*

---

[35] *Ministry of Science and Environment available at:* http://www.ghana.gov.gh/governing/ministires/social/environment.php. This *was formally the Ministry of environment, science and technology (MEST) it is still the same body and it performs the same functions, the technology ministry has been added to communication ministry making it the ministry of communications and technology*
[36] *Id.*

- *Setting standards and regulating activities with regard to the application of science and technology in managing the environment for sustainable development*
- *Promotion of activities needed to promote standards and policies required for planning and implementation of development activities*
- *Coordination, supervision, monitoring and evaluation of activities that support goals and targets sustainable development*

Through the Ministry, Ghana has ratified a number of Multilateral Environmental Agreements; this will strengthen international cooperation and linkages for better management of the environment and application of sound technologies. The ratification of these Multilateral Environmental Agreements has enabled Ghana to access financial support to protect its environment. It has also created environmental desks in various public institutions following the approval of mainstreaming environmental issues into national development programs and projects. The Ministry has developed a National Action Program to combat desertification.[37] This program has assisted in checking the downward movement of the desert in the Sahel. In addition, a National Biodiversity Strategy for Ghana has been launched. This strategy will be disseminated to various stakeholders and interest group in the country. The aim is to ensure effective conservation and management of the country's depleting biodiversity.

2. The Environmental Protection Agency (EPA)[38]

The Environmental Protection Agency replaced the Environmental Protection Council

---

[37] Environmental Action Plan, supra note 10 at 107
[38] See Environmental Protection Agency Act, 1994. Note ss. 30 repeals the law establishing the Environmental Protection Council and dissolves the council.

(EPC), established in 1974, following the United Nations Stockholm Conference on Human Environment. The EPC performed advisory, research and coordinating functions on the environment. Its functions as set out in section 2 of the Decree among other things, were to advice the government on environmental matters, coordinate the activities of all bodies concerned with environmental matters, conduct and promote investigations, studies, surveys, research and training of personnel relating to the improvement of the environment in Ghana. In addition, it also liaised with national and international bodies on environmental matters and undertook such studies and submit reports and recommendations on the environment at the behest of the government. Its greatest achievement was the publication of the volume 2 of Ghana Environmental Action Plan, which was a major policy initiative. Its major setback however, was the fact that it was merely an advisory body and therefore lacked any power to enforce its policies. This made it ill-suited to deal with the problems related to environment.[39]

Secondly, the creation of the Ministry of Environment cabinet under the Fourth Republican Constitution shifted the role of formulating environmental policies to the ministry hence the need to redefine the functions of the EPC to avoid duplication and unnecessary overlapping.[40]

The EPA has full mandate to regulate the environment and ensure implementation of government policies on the environment. The EPA is a corporate body with legal personality, capable of acquiring and holding property, capable of suing and being sued

---

[39] See George Sarpong, "From Stockholm to Rio: Some Ghanaian Responses to the problems of the Environment" 9 U.GH.L.J. (1994)
[40] See Memorandum to the Environmental Protection Act Bill, (1994) (enacted)

and capacity to enter into contracts.[41] The EPA does not only perform advisory, research and coordinating functions, it also has enforcement powers.[42]

The duties of the EPA are quite comprehensive and require huge amounts of resources to be effective. In line with this, Act 490 establishing the EPA makes provisions for a National Environmental Fund[43] to provide funding to the EPA's activities. The Fund is financed by grants from the government for the protection or improvement of the environment; Other funding sources include levies collected by the Agency in the performance of its functions; donations from the general public, institutions and organizations. Monies from the Fund are used for environmental education of the public, research, studies and investigations relating to the functions of the Agency and human resource development[44]. The Agency has power to request for an environmental impact assessment from any person planning to undertake a development project, which in the opinion of the Agency has or is likely to have effect on the environment. It also has power to impose fines for non-compliance of

---

[41] EPA Act supra ss., 1

[42] To advice the minister on the formulation of policies on all aspects of the environment and in particular make recommendations for the protection of the environment; to coordinate the activities of bodies concerned with the technical or practical aspect of the environment and serve as a channel of communication between such bodies and the ministry; to coordinate the activities of such bodies as it considers appropriate for the purposes of controlling the generation, treatment, storage, transportation and disposal of industrial waste; to secure in collaboration with such persons as it may determine, the control and prevention of discharge of waste into the environment and the improvement of the quality of the environment; to collaborate with such foreign and international agencies as the Agency considers necessary for the purpose of this Act to issue environmental permits and pollution abatement notices for controlling the volume, types, constituents and effects of waste discharges, emissions, deposits or other sources of pollutants and of substance which are hazardous or potentially dangerous to the quality of the environment or any segment of the environment; to prescribe standards and guidelines relating to the pollution of air, water, land and other forms of environmental pollution including the discharge of wastes and the control of toxic substances; to ensure compliance with any laid down environmental impact assessment procedures in the planning and execution of development projects, including compliance in respect of existing projects; to act in liaison and cooperation with District Assemblies and other bodies and institutions to control pollution and generally protect the environment. to conduct investigations into environmental issues and advice the minister thereon; to promote studies, research, surveys and analysis for the improvement and the protection of environment and the maintenance of sound ecological systems in Ghana;
to initiate and pursue formal and non-formal education programs for the creation of public awareness of the environment and its importance to the economic and social life of the country.
[43] EPA Act, supra ss. 16
[44] Id. at ss. 17

its orders. The functions of the EPA is in line with Ghana's commitments under many of the Multilateral Environmental Agreements it has acceded to, among them, are the Convention to Combat Desertification which calls for education and awareness creation of the general public on environmental hazards.

The EPA also works with other departments whose activities have a bearing on the environment to formulate and implement Ghana's environmental policies and programs. They are the Forestry Department; the National Energy Board; the Department of Parks and Gardens and the Water Resources Research Institute (WRRI). The EPA is also responsible for the coordinating of the NEAP by setting up inter- sectoral networks with the responsibility of implementing the NEAP. To achieve sustainable balance between economic growth and sound environmental management in Ghana, the EPA has adopted "An integrated environmental planning and management systems established on a broad base of public participation, efficient implementation of appropriate programs and technical services, giving good counsel on environmental management as well as effective and consistent enforcement of environmental laws and regulations. The EPA is an implementing Agency, a regulatory body and a catalyst for change towards sound environmental stewardship."[45] To achieve this, a number of policies have been outlined. They include the use of cost effective means to achieve environmental objectives and optimum sustainable yield in the use of resources and ecosystems; the use of incentives in addition, to regulatory measures and delegating decision-making and action to local governments. It also aims at adopting the principle of polluter pays for the cost of preventing and eradicating pollution, promote international cooperation, and grass

---

[45] *Environmental Protection Agency at a Glance,* supra note 33

root participation.[46]

3. The District Assemblies

In line with Ghana's policy on decentralization and its obligation under the Convention to Combat Desertification, the government has delegated to the District Assemblies (DAs) a role in implementation of its NEAP.[47] The role of the District Assemblies in environmental management is to serve as an organ through which national policies and programs on the environment will be translated into action at the local and district levels. In addition, their action programs will serve as vehicles for creating awareness at the grassroots levels of the complex interaction between development and environment in other to ensure improved quality of life for the people. In line with this, the District Assemblies have set up the Community Environmental Committees (CECs) through which its environmental programs will be carried out. District Environmental Management Committees (DEMCs) are to monitor and coordinate environmental protection activities to improve environmental quality in the local communities. The District Assemblies also liaise with the EPA to control pollution and curb bush fires, which is the main cause of desertification in the northern part of Ghana.[48] Their major source of funding is from the District Assembly's Common Fund, which is woefully inadequate considering the tasks they have to carry out.

---

[46] *Boon, supra note 11 at 34*
[47] *Environmental Action Plan supra note 10*
[48] *Boon, supra note 11 at 24-25*

4. The National Development Planning Commission (NDPC)

The National Development Planning Commission was established under Article 86 of the Ghanaian Constitution to formulate and advice the government on comprehensive national planning and development strategies and to ensure that planning and development programs are effectively carried out. It also plays an important role in monitoring, evaluation and control of national development programs, including making proposals for the protection of the environment.

C. Environmental Legislation in Ghana

This section will discuss some of the legislations, enacted to give effect to Ghana's obligations under the various Multilateral Environmental Agreements it has ratified. It must be noted that some legislations on the environment predated the Stockholm Conference; however these legislations were not adequate because they were sectoral in nature and therefore limited in scope. The most important factor that influenced recent environmental legislation in Ghana was the 1992 Rio Conference. The Brundtland Report,[49] the Rio declaration on Environment and Development and Agenda 21 contributed immensely to the enactment and amendment of several legislations to promote environmental quality.[50] As a result several legislations were enacted to address environmental problems in Ghana some of these legislations were also in place before

---

[49] See The Brundtland Report available at: http://www.brundtlandnet.com/brundtlandreport.htm
[50] Boon, supra note 11 at 27-28

Ghana ratified conventions addressing them; an example is the Wild Animal Preservation Act of 1962.

1. **The Convention on Wetlands of International Importance Especially as Waterfowl Habitats** *(also known as Ramsar)[51] was the first global effort to address wetlands which are among the most biological productive habitats in the world and very valuable when translated into monetary terms[52]. Fishes and other water resources depend on estuaries and other wetlands for their food, and breeding grounds. Wet lands also controls floods by maintaining water tables for agriculture, filtering water sources, checking shoreline erosion and providing abodes for species biodiversity.[53] The Ramsar Convention[54] was signed in 1971 in Ramsar, Iran mainly because of concerns in the 1960s over serious declines in the populations of migratory waterfowls and their habitats. This was brought to light by international conferences and research conducted by Wetland International, an NGO of International Waterfowls Resources Bureau. This Convention like others established an international framework for funding and monitoring wetland and imposed obligations on Parties to conserve wetlands. Ramsar now has about 123 Parties[55]. Ghana ratified Ramsar on February 22, 1988 and acceded to it on June 22, the same year. Ghana and other Contracting Parties have the responsibility to conserve wetlands by designating at least one wetland within their*

---

[51] *See Convention on Wetlands of International Importance Especially As Waterfowls Habitat, Feb. 2, 1971, U.N.T.S. 245; See also 1972, 11 I.L.M. 963 [hereinafter Ramsar Convention]*
[52] *Hunter, supra note 13 at 1028*
[53] *Id.*
[54] *Entered into force on December 21,1975*
[55] *Available at: http://www.ramsar.org/, List of International Wetlands*

territories for inclusion in a List of Wetlands of International Importance;[56] formulate and implement policies to promote conservation of wetlands included in the list;[57] promote conservation through the creation of nature reserves on wetlands;[58] encourage research, exchange of data and publications regarding wetlands;[59] endeavor through management to increase waterfowl population;[60] promote training of personnel competent in fields of wetland research, management; [61] to consult each other on implementation of its obligations assumed under the convention and ensure implementation through conferences every three years.[62]

A "wetland" is defined in the Convention[63] as an area of marsh, fen, peat land or water natural or artificial, temporary or permanent with water that is static or flowing, fresh, salt or brackish including areas of maritime water the depth of which at low tide does not exceed six meters. Wetlands are very important and this is reflective in the provisions of the convention. The Ramsar Convention required Parties to formulate and implement plans to promote the conservation of wetlands they have included in the List and as far as possible the "wise use" in their territories.

To implement Ghana's obligation under the Ramsar convention, the Wetland Management (Ramsar Sites) Regulations 1999 [64] was passed. It outlined the areas designated as Ramsar sites[65] and required the Minister for Land and Forestry to declare

---

[56] See art. 2(1)
[57] Id. art. 3 (1)
[58] Id. art. 4(1)
[59] Id. art. 4(3)
[60] Id. art. 4(4)
[61] Id. art. 4(5)
[62] Id. art. 6
[63] Id. art. I
[64] See Legislative Instrument, 1999 [hereinafter Ramsar Regulation]
[65] Ramsar Convention, supra note 51(this provision is in line with art. 2 of the Ramsar convention which requires a Party to designate suitable wetlands within its territory for inclusion in a List as wetland of international importance)

closed seasons during which certain activities such as fishing are prohibited and Section 3 vests the Minister with responsibility to designate core areas of Ramsar Sites to make for their effective management. The Director of the Wildlife Division of the Forestry publication of the dates of such closure in the gazette or mass media.[66] Commission or his authorized representative is supposed to demarcate the core area designated by the Minister within the Ramsar Site. For example, he is supposed to indicate by physical marking in the Ramsar site where litter may not be deposited, this he may do by educating the community members where the site is located. The Minister has the responsibility to approve areas in Ramsar Site where sand winning and quarrying activities take place, by publishing them in the gazette or through the media.[67] The District Assemblies are also involved in the Ramsar site management; they, in consultation with the Minister of Lands and Forestry authorize certain activities in the Ramsar site. This authorization is by way of enacting byelaws[68] prescribing customary and conservation practices, which are compatible with the Ramsar Convention and prescribed under this regulation.[69] The Director of the Wildlife Division determines the type of wise use activities permitted in core areas of a Ramsar Site for its sustainable utilization; and the conditions that will sustain the use of the resources under which the permitted wise use activities are carried out. The Regulation defines "wise use" as the "sustainable utilization for the benefit of mankind in a way compatible with the natural properties of the ecosystem." The commencement of any activity in a Ramsar site is to be preceded by a written approval by the designated official and it prohibits physical

---

[66] Id. at ss.1 &2
[67] Id. at ss. 4
[68] Bye-Laws in Ghana are made by District Assemblies by authority vested in them by the Constitution
[69] Ramsar Regulation, supra note 64 at ss 5

development in any designated Ramsar Site. It proscribe use of poisonous chemicals, explosive or any prohibited method for fishing, use of seine nets or other nets with mesh size below 25mm, fishing during the closed season or doing of any other act that is likely to have an adverse effect on the environment. Other activities prohibited under the Ramsar Regulations include: Removing woody vegetation or cultivating any portion in a core area except with the written consent of the Director of the Wildlife Division of the Forestry Commission given in consultation with the Committee of the District Assembly in charge of the environment and the natural resources; hunting, capturing harming or deliberately disturbing any wild animals including roosting, breeding and nesting birds, fledging, turtle or their eggs except as authorized by the official in charge; grazing livestock in and around bird nesting sites during nesting periods; starting bush fire within a distance of 1 kilometer from the boundary of a Ramsar site; or doing any other act to disturb the ecosystem.

For enforcement, section 8 makes the violation of any provision under the Regulation an offence, and prescribes punishment on summary conviction. Penalties range from 100,000 to 5 million cedis and even prison sentences. In addition to the fine or term of imprisonment, an offender convicted for causing damage to the environment shall pay for the cost of its rehabilitation as may be ordered by the court and the court for this purpose may consult the EPA. The police are empowered under the Regulation to confiscate any equipment, or tools from anyone arrested where the equipments have been used in contravention of the Regulation.[70]

The current Ghanaian practice is also in conformity with the obligations it assumed under the Ramsar convention. Following its ratification Ghana has designated certain

---

[70] Id. at ss. 9

areas as Ramsar Sites. A Ramsar site is defined to mean, " an area designated to be managed in accordance with the "wise use concept" of the Ramsar convention.[71] The following have been designated as Ramsar sites:

- The Densu Delta site located 11 kilometers west of Accra
- Sakumono Lagoon located at the west of Tema in the Greater-Accra Region the
- Keta Lagoon Complex covering all or portions of South Tongu, Akatsi, Ketu and Keta districts of the Volta Region
- Songhor Lagoon located within the Dangbe West District of the Greater-Accra Region
- Muni-Pomadzi site located within the Awuta/Effetua/Senya and Gomoa Districts of the Central Region

In addition, a National Wetlands Conservation and Management Strategy has been prepared to implement and manage these six Ramsar sites and others, which will be listed in the future. All the Ramsar Sites have been demarcated as management areas and management plans have been put in place. Management Committees, which include representatives, from the local communities are responsible for the management of the various Ramsar sites. Research and studies have also been conducted to obtain scientific information from these sites and an Ecological Monitoring Program has been completed. The National Wetlands Conservation and Management Strategy, has designated these wetland as tourist sites or observation posts and platforms are mounted for tourist to view these sites and their ecology around them. Sensitization programs on wetlands and their importance to the environmental, social and economic development of Ghana and

---

[71] Id. ss. 10

financial support has been given to the communities around these sites to undertake alternative income which are more friendly to the environment. Fishermen especially from various Ramsar sites have been assisted financially to obtain the right kind of fishing nets for fishing. This is because most of these fishermen use the wrong mesh or net size and so, catch fingerlings the effect of this practices defeats the whole idea of wise and sustainable use.

2. **Convention on International Trade in Endangered Species of Wild Fauna and Flora (1973)**[72] *was signed on March 3, 1973 in Washington D.C., United States of America. It was adopted to regulate global trade in threatened and endangered species by restricting the flow of extinct species across territorial borders. CITES places restriction based on the level of extinction. Thus, it classifies species by reference to their endangered status and places them into Appendices I, II, and III. CITES recognizes the rights of sovereign states over their natural resources and therefore treads carefully by only regulating species not within national borders but only regulates them when they enter the arena of international market. Ghana ratified CITES on November 14, 1975 and acceded to it on February 12, 1976. The system of Appendices is the core of CITES protection.*

Appendix I list species that are seriously endangered and may be affected by trade. Regulated under its Article III, Appendix I species including all sea turtles, tigers, cheetahs and all great apes etc. It may only be traded in if; both the exporting and importing countries issue permits and agree to the international trade. Importing and

---

[72] *See Convention on International Trade in Endangered Species, Mar. 3, 1973, 27 U.S.T. 1087; see also 12 I.L.M. 1085 [hereinafter CITES]*

exporting country's Scientific and Management Authorities must give their advice before issuing licenses and permits.

Appendix II lists species that are not yet threatened with extinction, but may become extinct if trade is not controlled and monitored to avoid exploitation incompatible with their survival. Appendix II lists over 25,000 species including Narwhal whales, Polar bears. Trade in these species requires the country to issue export permits only and not, import. It also requires advice from the country's scientific and management authorities[73] that, the export of the specimen were not obtained in breach of state laws and that method of shipment will not cause any harm or injury or involve any maltreatment to the animal.

Appendix III lists species that are already protected under a country's laws but, requires the cooperation of CITES parties to control its trade in the international market. Appendix III species are also the least threatened by trade. Appendix III does not require import permit neither does it require scientific authority.[74] However, the export of any specimen or species in Appendix III from any State, which has listed that species in Appendix III, requires export permit. The management authority of that country has to be satisfied that, the specimen were not obtained in violation of domestic laws and that measures will be taken to transport the specimen without causing any injury to them.[75] The convention also requires state parties to adopt appropriate measures to enforce provisions of the conventions and to prohibit trade in specimen that violates the convention. The Convention entered into force on July 1, 1975.

---

[73] See art. IV, para. 2 (a) (b) (c)
[74] Id. V, para. 2 (a) (b)
[75] Id.

3. **Convention on the Conservation of Migratory Species of Wild Animals**[76] was signed in Bonn, Germany on June 23, 1979. This Convention aimed at conservation and effective management of species of wild animals that move across territorial borders. The convention like CITES, categorize species into Appendices and requires contracting Parties to act appropriately to protect them. It requires parties that are range states of migratory species listed in its Appendix I to prohibit the taking of the animals and must act appropriately to conserve and restore habitats, prevent or minimize adverse activities, which seriously impede migratory species and endanger them.[77] Appendix II list migratory species which have an unfavorable conservation status and which require International cooperation by parties for their conservation and management and the restoration of them into a favorable conservation status or maintain them in such a status.[78] Ghana ratified this convention on January 19, 1988.

The relevant piece of Ghanaian legislation addressing wildlife is the Wild Animals Preservation Act, 1961[79]. This legislation was enacted before the CITES came into force however to some extent some of its provisions conforms to the provisions in CITES. The Wild Animals Preservation Act provides for the establishment of reserve, national parks and sanctuaries. It list species that are protected and regulates the hunting and trading in trophies. It provides for sanctions for violation of the Act[80]. In most cases, offenders have been prosecuted. Several pieces of regulations have been passed: the Conservation

---

[76] See United Nations Convention on Conservation of Migratory Species of Wild Animals, Bonn, June 23, 1979, 19 ILM15 [hereinafter Convention on Migratory Species]
[77] Id. art.V para. 4 &5
[78] Id. art.IV and V. These articles further provides that range states must conclude agreements to benefit these species and to keep the Secretariat regularly informed as to implementation measures.
[79] See Wild Animals Preservation Act of Ghana, 1961
[80] Id. at ss. 5

Regulations[81] and Wildlife Reservation Regulation[82]. The Conservation Regulations place a total ban on the hunting, capturing or destruction of such endangered species as chimps, lions, elephants crocodiles, parrots and turtles. This provision gives effect to provisions in article 6 of CITES which place total ban on trade in certain species and specimen. Schedule I of the Wild Animal Preservation Act list species under Appendix III of CITES. These include the palm squirrel, water chevrotain, spot-breasted Ibis, white-breasted guinea fowl and the marabou stock, among others. Hunting and collection of some species required permit and the Chief Game and Wildlife Officer may confiscate any equipment brought into any reserve which in his opinion is being used to commit any offence. License and authorization permit is required before hunting in certain kind species. Subsequent to these provisions, five national protected parks have been designated these are; the Mole, Digya which has species of manatee and dewless otter, Bui which covers catchments of the Black Volta, Bia and Nin-Suhien which has the rare white fronted guinea fowls. Two wildlife sanctuaries established in Owabi and Bomfiri, have the highly threatened bareheaded rock fowl. It is estimated that about 4% of Ghana's land surface has been designated as conservation areas[83].

The Ghana Wildlife has also adopted the Wildlife Development Plan to run between 1998-2003. The purpose is to embark upon intensive wildlife conservation training. Between 1992-1996, the government spent an estimated amount of US$15,909,750 on this program.[84] In Ghana, trade in Appendix I species is banned under the Regulations. Therefore trade in Appendix I species like the elephant, crocodiles, lions and leopards as

---

[81] See Wild Animals Preservation Regulation L.I. 685 as amended by L.I. 1283
[82] See L.I. 710 as amended by L.I. 1284

well as their parts for ornamental purposes is prohibited.[85] Trade in Appendix II species is allowed subject to the grant of licenses and certificates. The exporter is required to get a clearance from the importing country before the species can be shipped from Ghana without such clearance the export will not be allowed.[86] In addition, trades in Appendix III species is also allowed but unlike the provisions in CITES, the authorities in Ghana insist on import and export permits. There are certain species of reptile in respect of which certain countries have expressed reservations about them for example, chameleons and pythons. The Wildlife Division of the Forestry Commission set import quotas for these species and communicate this information to the CITES secretariat in Chatelaine, Geneva. For instance the export quotas for chameleon gracilis for the year 2001 was 1500; for Kinixys homeana for the same year was 340; for python regius was 7000.[87] There is also cooperation with other states. In August 2001, a sub-regional workshop proposed by Ghana was held in Accra to foster cooperation in the sub-region, to discuss the formalization of trade in endangered species across the borders. Even though CITES is being strictly implemented[88] the penalties imposed are insignificant and does nothing to deter offenders.

---

[83] See E.O.Asibey, "Effective Policies for the Management of Game and Wildlife Resources of Ghana" 1980 (Unpublished report)
[84] See Ghana's Wildlife Development Plan (1992)
[85] CITES, supra note 72 at art. III
[86] See Id.
[87] See Wildlife Division Document No. WD/A 244/Vol 13 November 14th 2000 addressed to the CITES secretariat in Geneva. Note a scientific basis for the quotas has to be provided. The quotas are set after research has been conducted by the Wildlife Division liaising with the Institute of Renewable Resources and CITES officials. The research is sponsored by the CITES Secretariat. The quotas is based on the number of species both male and female ratio, their gestation period, reproduction pattern, food requirements and their infant mortality rate. (Unpublished report)
[88] There are instances where Ghanaians have been fined and imprisoned for engaging in illegal trading of endangered species. For example, two Americans were imprisoned for illegally exporting parrots

4. United Nation Convention on the Law of the Sea, 1982[89] *was signed in Montego Bay in 1982 and entered into force in 1994. UNCLOS established an International regime for ocean governance by providing broad rules and direction to guide general behavior concerning the sea and its living resources. UNCLOS set out the general rights and the obligations of states for the sustainable use of marine living resources. It recognizes the sovereignty of coastal states over their coastal waters and their territorial sea and further extends up to a 12 nautical miles from the base line.* [90] *Coastal states have the sole discretion to enact laws and regulations to exploit and conserve living resources in their territorial waters*[91]. *UNCLOS also established for the first time the Exclusive Economic Zone (EEZ), which has now become a feature of International maritime law. It recognizes the International nature of the EEZ regime and hence makes provision for participation of other states in exploitation of marine living resources. It enjoins coastal states to permit other states access to the surplus of the allowable catch.*[92] *However, this is subject to the sole discretion of coastal states. Coastal states have the right to determine the allowable fisheries catches and it is required to adopt measures that will conserve rather than exploit them. This they may do in cooperation with International Bodies. Coastal states establishing the EEZ have a duty among other things to also take into account the best scientific evidence available to it for the purpose of ensuring through proper conservation and management measures that*

---

[89] See United Nations Convention on the Law of the Sea, Montego Bay, Dec. 10,1982,12 I.L.M. 1261 [hereinafter UNCLOS]
[90] Id. art. III.
[91] Id. art. XXI, para. C
[92] Id. art. 61-70

maintenance of living resources in the EEZ is not endangered by over exploitation.[93] Ghana signed the UNCLOS on December 10, 1982 and ratified it on June 7, 1983.

The Maritime Zones (Delimitation) Law [94] and the Fisheries Law [95] were enacted to give effect to the provisions of UNCLOS dealing with the delimitation of the territorial sea, the contiguous zones and the Exclusive Economic Zone.

The Maritime Zones (Delimitation) Law has no specific provision on conservation of marine resources. The Fisheries law on the other hand, applies throughout Ghana's declared 200 miles EEZ this, is to give effect to the provisions of the UNCLOS which grants sovereign states the right over their territorial sea for purpose of exploring, conserving and managing their marine resources.[96] The Fisheries Law prohibits the building of motor vessels without license and the design of such vessels are made subject to the authorization of the Shipping Commissioner who on completion of the vessel will issue a seaworthiness certificate before it could be offered for sale. The law also bans the operation without license of any fishing craft within the coastal waters of Ghana for purposes of fishing or in connection with any fishing activity. An innovation under the law is the establishment of the Fisheries Monitoring, Control, Surveillance and Enforcement Unit[97]. This Unit monitors and controls all fishing operations within Ghana's coastal waters. It has powers and privileges of the police to enforce the law. Under the law, it has wide powers to arrest any person or fishing craft where there is a reasonable suspicion that any act has been done by the person or in relation to the craft in contravention of any provisions of the law or any regulation made pursuant to it. It has

---
[93] Id.
[94] See The Maritime Zones (Delimitation) Law of Ghana, 1986
[95] See Fisheries Law of Ghana, 1991
[96] UNCLOS, supra note 89, at art. 145

power to board any fishing craft to inspect any license or other document issued in relation to such fishing craft and to search and examine fishing gear or other apparatus carried on or in such fishing craft. It can require the owner or person in charge of a fishing craft to exhibit his/her fishing gear or apparatus or catch and enter any premises ashore where there is reasonable suspicion of any contravention of this law and inspect such premises, catch, fishing gear or other apparatus of fishing craft involved in such contravention.[98] On enforcement, the law imposes penalty for contravention of the provision. The penalty ranges from 50, 000 to US$150,000 in case of infringement by foreign owned or registered vessels.

5. MARPOL[99] comprise of the 1973 London Convention on oil pollution and the Protocol of 1978 Relating to the International Convention for the Prevention of Pollution from Ships. It regulates operational discharge and unintentional release of pollutants such as oil, garbage, plastic and sewage from vessels. It consist of six annexes, each with regulations controlling specific type of vessel source pollution among them are oil pollution and noxious liquid substances in bulk (which are specified in Annexes I and II and mandatory for all parties). Apart from its discharge requirements, it required that all new ships be built with Segregated Ballast Tanks, special tanks for holding oily residues, oil-water separating equipments, filters. It limits the size of cargoes to be carried by tanks. In addition, it prohibited the discharge of oil in areas like the Mediterranean Sea, Black Sea, and Gulf Waters among others.

---

[97] *Hereinafter The Unit*
[98] *Fisheries Law supra note 94 at ss. 11 & 12*
[99] *See London International Convention for the Prevention of Pollution from Ships (MARPOL), Nov. 2, 1973 12 ILM 1319*

Programs in place concerning marine environmental protection in Ghana include: Ghana Environmental Resource Management Project; Gulf of Guinea Large Marine Ecosystem Project; Establishment of a Protected Wetland Ecosystem on the Coast; National Oil Spill Contingency Plan; Monitoring, Compliance and Surveillance of the Marine Environment Project and Increased public education on sound coastal and marine environmental practices. The EPA as part of the ministry of Science and Environment is the agency charged with the responsibility for dealing with oil spills in Ghana. It liaises with the ministry of Transport and Communication, and the naval operation is required to provide on-scene commander to coordinate military in spills reconnaissance and clean up.[100] The Contingency Plan gives containment and recovery as the preferred option for oil spills response, dispersant use, however is listed as being both feasible and desirable, in some cases clean up involves annual shoreline cleaning because of the predominant on shore winds for much of the year.[101] It provides for burning, landfill, recycling recovered oil at refinery or re-use in the industry. The Plan has very little equipment facility to respond to oil spills. Ghana has not experienced any major oil spill in its coastal waters, the main oil spills which are very minor are the ones from its main refinery in Tema and from the two major ports Tema and Takoradi. Ghana has ratified some of the Annexes to the MARPOL,[102] the others are nor yet in force.

6. Convention on Biological Diversity[103] *was open for signature during the Rio Conference in 1992 and entered into force on December 29, 1993. Over 144 states including almost all African countries are parties to this convention. The CBD is a*

---

[100] *See Ghana's Environmental Profile available at:*
 http://www.un.org/esa/agenda21/natlinfo/countr/ghana/natur.htm
[101] *Id.*
[102] *MARPOL supra note 99 at IV & VI*

framework convention, which is broad in scope covering virtually all aspect of biodiversity. Even though it is a framework convention it enjoined parties among other things to develop national plans, strategies or programs for the conservation and the sustainable use of biodiversity; inventory and monitor the use of biodiversity within their jurisdiction; identify and regulate destructive activities and integrate consideration of biodiversity into national policies and decision making.[104] It further provides that contracting Parties should establish In-situ and Ex-situ conservation measures for biodiversity; cooperation in providing financial and other support to developing countries[105], introduction of appropriate procedures requiring environmental impact assessment of proposed projects that are likely to have significant adverse effects on biological diversity with a view to avoiding or minimizing such effects and, where appropriate, allow for public participation in such procedures and exchange of information.[106] Ghana has ratified the CBD convention. Activities to implement the Biodiversity Convention include the preparation of a Biodiversity country study, a Biodiversity strategy and Action plan, a program for increasing the awareness of the need for sustainable management of biological resources; financial, human, material and institutional capacity building to support conservation of biodiversity; and participation of communities in the management of biological resources.

7. **United Nation Convention to Combat Desertification in Those Countries Experiencing Serious Draught and/or Desertification, Particularly in Africa**[107] was adopted after intense negotiations on June 17,1994 and became effective on December

---

[103] See Convention on Biological Diversity, Rio Dec. 29, 1993, 18 ILM 818 [hereinafter CBD] [104] Id. art. 6 para. a & b
[105] Id. art.8 & 9
[106] Id. art.14

26,1996. It has received 172 ratification, as of February 2001 (Ghana ratified CCD on December27, 1996). The object of the CCD is to combat desertification and mitigate the effects of drought in countries affected especially Africa through effective action at all level, supported by international co-operation and partnership arrangements in the framework of an integrated approach consistent with Agenda 21.

The CCD in various ways differs from other Multilateral Environmental Agreements in the sense that, it does not place substantive emphasis on state actions but rather stress on popular participation in developing and implementing plans to combat desertification. It emphasis on a " bottom up" approach, which stress on the need for government to channel authority and resources down to local communities, land users and local NGOs. Under the CCD, affected parties are enjoined to give high priority to combating desertification and effects of droughts, address socio-economic causes of desertification as well as promote the participation of women and NGOs in combating desertification.[108] Developed countries are required to actively support either individually or jointly, the efforts of affected developing country parties, especially, countries in Africa, to combat desertification. In addition, they are to provide substantial financial assistance and other forms of support to assist African countries to develop and implement long terms plans and strategies to combat desertification and mitigate effects of drought.[109] Article 9 requires affected parties to develop and implement National Action Plans (NAPs), integrating any existing programs to ensure success.

---

[107] See United Nations Convention to Combat Desertification, June 17, 1994, 331 ILM 1328 [hereinafter CCD]
[108] Id. art. 5
[109] Id. art 6 para. a & b

Article 10 establishes the framework for developing NAPs by relying on "participatory mechanism". This mechanism requires the participation of the government, local communities and land users to work together in combating desertification and eradicate poverty (reflecting the coupling of environment and development at UNCED). NAPs require incorporation of long-term strategies and priorities for affected areas with special emphasis on natural resource conservation, drought contingency plans, and improved early warning systems. It further allows for modification and flexibility at local levels to cope with different socio-economic, biological and geo-physical conditions giving particular attention to preventive measures, and strengthening institutional framework and review of progress report on implementation.[110] This is a means of reviewing implementation and addressing poor issues of implementation.

Article 19 provides guidelines for capacity building to ensure effective implementation, article 20 provides that financial resources should be made available to the program by parties with help from developed countries and 21 establishes a financial mechanism to be made available to affected countries for implementation. For effective implementation, it established a "Global Mechanism" to identify and channel resources to developing countries. The Mechanism is to ensure effective funding of programs to combat desertification by coordinating and facilitating desperate aid programs.[111] The CCD prescribes the rehabilitation, conservation and sustainable management of land and water resources. Ghana seeks to effectively achieve these objectives through a system of bush-fire controls.[112]

---

[110] Id. art.10
[111] Id. art.21; the activities of the Mechanism is to create inventory of available multilateral and bilateral aid programs as well as to encourage innovative ways to raise funds and secure financial assistance. [112] Sarpong, supra at 30 at 27

The Control and Prevention of Bush fires Law[113] addresses the problem of bush fires. Applying the command and control approach as usual, the law prohibits the setting up of bush fires for any purpose and contravention of the law attracts a fine, imprisonment, or both. The law in addition, provides for establishment of bushfire control sub-committees within each District Assembly and they are responsible for drawing up and executing programs aimed at ensuring adequate prevention, control and monitoring of bushfires as well as creating awareness of the dangers and effects of bushfires through public education programs. Fire volunteer squad under the law, to assist the District Assemblies in the performance of their functions has also been established. The enactment of the Law has increased the level of awareness about dangers of bush fires and this has further reduced the incidents of uncontrolled fires.[114]

8. The International Tropical Timber Agreement[115] was ratified by Ghana on March 9, 1985 and it provided for the establishment of an International Tropical Timber Organization to administer its provisions and supervise the operation of the agreement, through the International Tropical Timber Council established under article 6 of the Agreement. The Ghanaian government has enacted several pieces of legislation: the Forest Protection Decree[116]; the Economic Plants Protection Decree[117]; and the Concession Act of 1962. The Forest Commission Act[118] is responsible for the regulation, management and utilization of forest resources. The Timber Resources Management

---

[113] See Bush fires Law, No. 229 1990, (GH)
[114] See Kotey "Land and Tree and Rural Development Forestry in Northern Ghana" (1993-95) 19 U.GH.L.J. p. 102
[115] See International Tropical Timber Agreement, Jan. 23, 1993, 33 I.L.M. 1041
[116] See Forest Protection Decree of Ghana, 1974
[117] See Economic Plant Protection Decree of Ghana, 1979,
[118] See The Forest Commission Act of Ghana, 1993

Act[119] and other forest policy have been adopted to give effect to the International Tropical Agreement as well as Ghana's obligations under the Biodiversity Convention[120]. The Timber Resource Management Act establishes the Timber Utilization Contract (TUC). This is a contract development and specification procedure, which requires seeking out the opinions and wishes of the community that owns the lands, regarding the area under contract, and the forest management operation. It requires a submission by the contractor of a Contract Operation Plan to address harvesting operation and how to address environmental impacts and the extent of involvement of the local communities. It calls for the right of landowners whose lands are within the contract area to veto harvesting within their lands or to require compensation for any damage caused by the felling of the timber. Further, a new approach has been adopted by the Forestry Ministry-the strategic forest management planning, which aims at expanding the possibility of greater and direct landowner and community involvement in decision-making and management of reserves, and of a more equitable sharing of benefits with the affected communities. This project is underway on a pilot basis and will be further developed in the course of the ongoing Natural Resources Management Program (NRMP).[121] This is a step in the right direction because the earlier forest laws and decree give little or no place for the land owners and the local communities who had no voice in the management of forest resources. The Timber Resources Management incorporates some of the principles in the Biodiversity Convention and the 1993 Tropical Timber Agreement by giving local communities stronger and greater participation in forest management, which is very necessary to ensure sustainable management. This is also

---

[119] See The Timber Resources Management Act of Ghana, 1999
[120] CBD supra note 103

a Declaration, which provides that "indigenous people and their communities; and other local communities, have a vital role in environmental management and development because of their knowledge and traditional practices. States should recognize and duly support their identity, culture and interest and enable their effective participation in the achievement of sustainable development"[122]

9. **The Vienna Convention for the Protection of the Ozone Layer**[123] was the first international agreement to address Chlorofluorocarbons (CFCs). It called for countries to take appropriate steps to protect the ozone layer and established international mechanism for research, monitoring and exchange of information. With very little information about the scale of CFCs production in developing countries, it was hoped this data would form the basis for establishing a global production baseline. The Vienna Convention does not identify any chemicals as ozone depleting substances instead, in a non-threatening description, the annex listed chemicals thought to have the potential to modify the chemicals and physical properties of the ozone layer. The Vienna Convention however, does not make any binding resolution, instead it called for a meeting of the Conference of the Parties to work towards a establishing a legally binding protocol to specifically address controls[124].

10. **The Montreal Protocol on Substances That Deplete the Ozone Layer**[125] got more participation from countries than Vienna Convention and this was the result of the discovery of the "ozone hole" by British scientist (it received over 60 participation from countries, industrial and environmental groups and wide media coverage). The Protocol

---

[121] Sarpong, supra note 30 at p23
[122] Rio Declaration supra note 2
[123] See Vienna Convention for the Protection of the Ozone Layer Mar. 22, 1985, 26 I.L.M. 1529 [hereinafter Vienna Convention]

froze production and consumption levels of CFCs upon ratification, and set in place a reduction schedule for CFCs calling for a 5% reduction by 1998 of CFCs consumption. It defined a country's consumption rate based on a total of its production, imports and exports.

There is no specific legislation in Ghana to give effect to the provisions and principles in the Ozone Layer Convention[126] and its Protocol[127] however, the government has adopted a strategy to phase out the use of Ozone Depleting Substances (ODS) in accordance with the ODS phase out schedule for article 5 countries under the Montreal Protocol.[128] To ensure the phase out, the government has focus on the refrigeration sector which consumes about 98% of the total ODS consumption in Ghana, by providing training programs for technicians in code of Good Practice in refrigeration; formulation of projects especially in the foam sector and awareness creation in all other sectors that produce ODS. Ghana has both short- term and long- term goals concerning reduction of greenhouse gas emissions. This is through; increasing greenhouse sinks by promoting afforestation, management of degraded land and Agro-forestry. Mitigating Ozone depletion and trans boundary air pollution efforts include implementation of programs and projects to phase out Chlorofluorocarbons (CFCs) in Ghana by 2010 and awareness creation to encourage Ghanaian industries to change over to Ozone friendly alternatives. The government is also carrying out monitoring programs and is encouraging users of refrigeration units to patronize Ozone friendly equipment.[129] Even though Ghana is not

---

[124] See art. 6
[125] Montreal Protocol, supra note 15
[126] Ozone Convention supra note 53
[127] Montreal Protocol, supra
[128] Id.
[129] See Ghana Environmental Profile available at
http://www.un.org/esa/agenda21/natlinfo/countr/ghana/natur.htm

directly involved in the chemical analysis or measurements of emissions of ozone depleting substances, it has nevertheless seen a reduction in the quantity of ODS imported. Since 1999, its current consumption stand at 43.65 tones as compared to 101.4 tones in 1991.[130] The national ambient air quality monitoring results indicate that air quality in Ghana's urban centers is generally good as most monitoring stations do not capture any disturbing levels of gaseous emissions thus, the only set back is lack of legislation for[131] ODS to sustain these efforts and to give it the legal force it needs.

With the assistance of Global Environment Facility (GEF), a National Climate Change project organized by the EPA has helped to promote climate change policy dialogue among government, NGOs, academic and business communities. This dialogue is intended to foster understanding of climate change issues and their linkages to national development agenda.

In furtherance of this cost-effective policy options for abatement of greenhouse gases, adaptation strategies have been developed for the agricultural, industrial, energy, forestry and waste sectors. The Ozone-Depleting substances (ODS) phase out project is aimed at promoting and implementing policies and programs to phase-out the consumption of ozone depleting substances, mainly CFCs by 2010. The project has led to about 70% reduction in the country's ODS consumption which is far ahead of allowable phase-out requirement of 50% reduction by the year 2005 stipulated by the Montreal Protocol.[132]

---

[130] Id.

[131] There are no specific Statutes regulating ODS in Ghana.

[132] Montreal Protocol, supra note 15; see also UNDP Ghana –Energy Environment, available at: http://www.UNDP.Ghana-Energy Environment.htm

Ghana has ratified numerous Regional Conventions within African and the sub-region. Most of these Regional environmental Conventions build upon and formalize Multilateral Environmental Conventions for effective implementation. However, several of these Agreements have failed because of inadequate financial mechanism to facilitate implementation. It is important to mention a few of these agreements and to note how their implementation will ensure sustainable use and preservation of biodiversity in Africa.

11. The 1968 African Convention on the Conservation of Nature and Natural

Resources[133] was the first environmental agreement under OAU. It sought to encourage individual and joint action for the conservation, utilization and development of natural resources for present and future welfare of mankind. State Parties were required to adopt measures to ensure conservation, utilization and development of soil, water, flora and fauna in accordance with scientific principles and with due regard to the best interest of the people.[134] They were also required to take effective measures to conserve and improve the soil and to control erosion and land use; establish policies to conserve, utilize and develop water use; protect flora and fauna and ensure its best utilization, including the management of forest and control burning, land clearing and overgrazing.[135] Ghana ratified this convention on November 14, 1975 and it entered into force for Ghana on February 12, 1976. No specific legislation has been enacted to give effect to this Convention, the principles of this Convention runs through various projects undertaken in Ghana.

---

[133] See African Convention on the Conservation of Nature and Natural Resources, Sept. 15,1968, 1001 UNTS 3
[134] See Id. art. II
[135] Id. art. IV, V, &VI

12. The Bamako Convention on the Ban of Import into Africa and the Control of Trans boundary Movement and Management of Hazardous Wastes within Africa[136] *was signed by all 51-member states of OAU on January 1991 in Bamako, Mali. The Convention which entered into force on April 22, 1998 bans the import of hazardous waste produced outside Africa. This convention was negotiated because African countries felt that the provisions in the Basel Convention[137] was not stringent enough and that it failed to address adequately three important problems: how to control shipments of toxic wastes; how to address inadequate disposal by importing state; and how to address the issue of bribery and forgery. Bamako Convention requires parties to ban under their₃ laws the importation of hazardous waste generated outside Africa. It requires parties to adopt laws making it illegal to dump hazardous waste into their territorial waters, exclusive economic zone and continental shelf.[138] It enjoined parties to create national bodies to act as watchdog or "Dump watch" and impose criminal penalties on offenders. Unfortunately, Ghana has not ratified this convention.*

D. Environmental Impact Assessment (EIA)

Environmental Impact Assessment is one of the most important conservation principles that grew with international environmental law. This concept describes a process that yields a statement to be used in guiding decision-making in relation to planned human activities that affects the environment. Environmental impact assessment if carried out should provide decision-makers with information on environmental consequences of proposed programs and policies. It provides a mechanism for ensuring the participation

---

[136] *See Bamako Convention on the Ban of the Import into Africa and the Control of Trans boundary Movements and Management of Hazardous Waste within Africa, 1991, 30 I.L.M 775*
[137] *See Basel Convention on the Control of Tran boundary Movements of Hazardous Wastes and their Disposal, Mar. 22, 1989, 28 I.L.M. 657*

of potentially affected persons in the decision-making process. The requirement of environmental impact assessment is found in several international agreements and is very important in implementation. For instance, Principle 17 of the Rio Declaration[139] provides that "environmental impact assessment, as a national instrument, shall be undertaken for the proposed activities that are likely to have a significant adverse impact on the environment and are subject to the decision of a competent national authority."[140]

This principle recognizes the importance of environment impact assessment to the maintenance of general environment standards and is central to preventive environmental management in Ghana. The Environment Impact Assessment Regulation[141] was passed to give effect to this principle and makes it mandatory. EIA was required for new investments in the pre-Rio period; however it was voluntary and therefore lacked the necessary force and sanction. The EIA Regulation provides that no person shall commence any activity or undertaking unless that undertaking has been registered with the EPA and the appropriate permit has been issued especially where the activity has or is likely to have adverse effect on the environment or public health.[142]

The first schedule in the Regulation list agricultural and related activities including: livestock farms, fruit and other vegetable farms, fishing and trapping, services incidental to fishing like fish breeding, logging and forestry, mining, sand quarries and sand winning, crude and natural gas production facilities, manufacturing and construction. Schedule two, list undertaking for which EIA is mandatory these include:

---

[138] See art. 4 para. 1 & 2 (a)
[139] Rio supra note 2
[140] Id.
[141] See Environmental Assessment Regulation of Ghana, 1999 (amended)
[142] Id. at ss 1

- *Land development for agricultural purposes not less than 40 hectares, agricultural programs which will necessitate the resettlement of 20 families or more;*
- *Construction of all airports or airstrips as well as the enlargement of existing airports or airstrips;*
- *Construction of dams, drainage of wetland and irrigation schemes;*
- *Coastal land reclamation and dredging of bars and estuaries;*
- *Construction and expansion of fishing harbors and land based aquatic undertakings*
- *Conversion of hill forest land to other land use, conversion of forest land to other land use and logging*
- *Human settlement development and housing projects*
- *Production of chemical where production capacity of each product or combination of product is more than 100 tones per day, production of aluminum, copper, non-metallic cement, iron and sheet, shipyard and pulp and paper*
- *Mining and processing of minerals and quarries*
- *Oil and gas fields development, construction on shore and off shore pipelines, construction of oil and gas separation, processing and storage facilities*
- *Waste treatment and disposal management*
- *Water supply;*
- *Power generation and transmission activities*

The regulation has a retrospective effect on activities which were undertaken before the commencement of the regulation and requires registration and permit as well. EIA is defined as "the process for the orderly and systematic evaluation of a proposal including its alternatives and objectives and its effect on the environment including the mitigation and management of those effects: the process extends from the initial concept of the proposal through implementation to completion, and where appropriate, decommissioning."[143] A person undertaking any of the above mention project is required to submit an application to the EPA after paying an application fee as determine by the EPA and has submitted any other information on the undertaking to the EPA. The EPA upon receipt of the application must conduct an initial assessment by screening the application taking into account: the location, size and likely output of the project, the technology intended to be used, the concern of the general population, land use and any other factors relevant to the project or undertaking. The report by the applicant must indicate any environmental, health and safety impact of the project, a clear commitment to avoid any adverse environmental effect, a clear commitment to address unavoidable environmental and health impacts and steps necessary for their reduction.[144] The EPA issues a screening report on the application by approving, objecting, requiring submission of a preliminary environmental report or requiring a submission of an environmental impact statement.[145] Where it approves the application at an initial assessment, it must register the undertaking and issue a permit to that effect. On the other hand, where the EPA objects the application, the screening report will serve as a non-acceptance of the application and the project will not be commenced or where it is in existence, it will, with immediate effect be discontinued. The regulation also allows the EPA to approve the application and requires the submission of a preliminary report or an environmental

---
[143] Id. at ss 30
[144] Id. at ss. 4& 5
[145] Id. at ss. 6

impact statement.[146] The regulation defines an environmental impact statement as "a document prepared by an applicant to present the case for the assessment of his proposal as part of the EIA process."[147] The regulation requires the environmental impact statement to address the following issues:

- Concentration of pollutants in environmental media including air, water and land from mobile to fixed sources
- Any direct ecological changes resulting from such pollutants, concentrations as they relate to communities, habitats, flora and fauna
- Alteration in ecological processes such as transfer of energy through food chains, decomposition and bio-accumulation which could affect any community, habitats or species of flora and fauna
- Ecological consequences of direct destruction of existing habitats from activities such as dumping of waste and vegetation clearance and fillings
- Noise and vibrations levels
- Odors

Change in social, cultural and economic patterns[148]

The applicant is required to publish the statement in the media, to the relevant ministry and make it available for inspection by the public.

The EIA regulation also provides for public hearings in respect of applications where there is an adverse public reaction to environmental impact statement and a further

---

[146] Id. at ss. 7 (This shall be communicated within 25 days from the date of the receipt of the application for the environmental permit)
[147] Id. at ss 30
[148] Id. at ss.14

review of the statement after the hearing.[149] This participatory mechanism is line with the CCD[150], which calls for involvement of local communities.

Environmental Impact Statement review is very important, in terms of its implications for sound decision-making and the sustainability of development activities. In this regard, the Ghana EIA procedures provides for the involvement of stakeholders in the assessment and review of proposed undertakings. This is achieved through a number of mechanisms, particularly the holding of public hearings. During public hearings within the context of the Ghana EIA processes, stakeholders and proponents are brought together in a forum to express their opinions and offer suggestions on a proposed undertaking in order to influence the decision-making process. This process has been applied selectively in

Ghana. The environmental permit is valid for a period of eighteen months when issued and can be suspended cancelled or revoked at any time. This is a very comprehensive piece of legislation, which requires both the financial resources and trained personnel in the field to adequately carry out and enforce it.

NGOs play important roles in environmental implementation. The degree of their participation in policy process and how well these groups organize themselves is very critical.[151] Under the coordination of the National Union of Environmental Non-Governmental Organizations (NUENGO), NGOs including Friends of the Earth, Network of Environmental NGOs, New Initiative Conservation, Green earth and the

---

[149] Id. at ss. 18 after a further review the EPA if not satisfied with the environmental impact statement, the applicant shall be notified in writing and shall be required to submit a revised environmental impact statement or to conduct further studies. Where environmental impact statement is acceptable the applicant shall be communicated in writing and the requisite environmental permit shall be issued to the applicant upon receipt of 8 hard copies of the approved environmental impact statement and a copy on a floppy diskette. At section 19
[150] CCD supra note 107 at art. 10
[151] See Edith Brown Weiss & Harold K. Jacobson (eds.): Engaging Countries: Strengthening Compliance with International Environmental Accords, 32 (1998)

Ghana Wildlife Society have registered with the EPA.[152] Their main activities include environmental education and communication through workshops and seminars, publishing and disseminating information on the environment to the public, putting pressure on government projects that are likely to have adverse impact on the environment, undertaking afforestation projects like tree planting exercise and wildlife conservation.[153] They are however, less active in Ghana because they are not well organize, and they have few memberships and are under considerable financial and technical constraint. Thus, they are neither able to play their role of pressuring the government to increase implementation nor are they able to complement the enforcement efforts of the government.

The environmental legislations discussed above are not exhaustive, there are various legislations on the environment however, those mentioned addresses Ghana's commitments under International law.

Research has shown that even though Ghana has acceded to most of Multilateral Environmental Agreements especially, the ones on Biodiversity. It has done very little to satisfy the requirement of domesticating them into legislation for them to have a binding effect in Ghana. Even though there is in existence constitutional, [154]

---

[152] See JICA country profile on environment available at:
http://www.jica.go.jp/English/global/env/profiles/e99gha.pdf
[153] Id.
[154] The Constitution of Ghana does not vest any environmental rights to the citizens. However, some of its provisions address the issue. For instance, Article 37(9) of the Constitution enjoins the state to take appropriate measure to protect and safeguard the natural environment for posterity; and to seek co-operation with other states and bodies for the purposes of protecting the wider international environment for mankind.

institutional and legislative framework, they have failed to address environmental problems and effectively implement Ghana's commitments under international law.[155]

---

[155] Sarpong, supra at 30

CHAPTER IV: OBSTACLES TO IMPLEMENTATION IN GHANA

Many factors account for the existing gaps in the legislative and institutional framework for environmental management and implementation in Ghana. They include: inadequate legislation and policy frame-work for implementation; financial constraint; lack of qualified personnel and expertise to assist in policy formulation; lack of in-depth understanding of contents of Multilateral Environmental Agreements; lack of public awareness and education and lack of adequate data and information system.

As noted above Ghana has acceded to more than thirty-five international conventions on the environment. However, these ratifications have not been adequately implemented through legislation. Article 73 of the Constitution[156] enjoins the Government to conduct its international relations in consonance with the acceptable principles of public international law and diplomacy in a manner consistent with the national interest of Ghana, to promote respect for international law and treaty obligations; and adhere to the principles and ideals of the U.N Charter and those of other international bodies and institutions of which Ghana is a member. In view of these provisions, Ghana has not lived up to its international obligation. Apart from failing to ratify some major international conventions, the ones already ratified have not been adequately implemented[157]. There are no legislation regulating discharge of ODS, governing air quality standards, control of emissions from industrial processes to fulfill its obligations

---

[156] *Ghana Constitution, supra note 154 at ch. VIII art 73*
[157] *See George Sarpong, International Environmental Law and the Ghanaian Courts, 6 (2000) (Unpublished paper)*

under the Montreal Protocol[158] and waste into water bodies, river or the marine environment.

The Oil in Navigable Waters Act of 1964[159], which was enacted to give effect to Ghana's obligations under OILPOL Convention, does not serve any useful purpose because it is obsolete. Even though Ghana has also ratified the MARPOL 73/78[160], it has not enacted it into legislation thus, there is no legislation regulating vessel source pollution in Ghana. Where legislations have been enacted, they are either inadequate to address the environmental problems or they contradicts the provisions of the international environmental convention from which it derives it source. For instance, the Fisheries Law 1991[161] which was enacted to give effect to UNCLOS[162] provisions on conservation of living resources through a system of prohibition and licensing violates some provisions of UNCLOS.[163] It imposes a prison term of 15years and confiscation of fishing equipment used in the commission of the offence. This is contrary to article 73, which provides for only monetary sanctions for violations in the EEZ. The Ghanaian courts in the Ajax Case[164] applied this provision and ordered the confiscations of the offenders' equipments. The decision has been criticized as been in excess of the monetary penalty prescribed by the provisions in UNCLOS.[165] In addition, UNCLOS[166]

---

[158] Montreal Protocol supra note 15
[159] See The Oil in Navigable Waters Act of Ghana, 1964
[160] MARPOL, supra note 99
[161] Fisheries Law, supra note 94
[162] UNCLOS supra note 89
[163] Id. art. 73
[164] See the People v. Captain Papaikonoumou Nikolaos Panayotis Stafilis; Chatzigeourgiou Nikolao Theodoreos Arqoudelis; Ajax III; Ajax Shipping Company (Greece). Case No. 85/89. March 1989. This was a decision of the then National Public Tribunal, Accra
[165] See George Sarpong Ghana's Fisheries Legislation: The Ajax Case and the United Nations Conventions on the Law of the Sea 17 RGL 289 (1989-90)
[166] UNCLOS supra note 89

further imposes obligation on state parties to enact IMO rules[167] into national legislations to regulate vessel source pollution, but Ghana as of date has not enacted any IMO rules into legislation even though, Ghana is a both a port and a flag state.

The fines imposed by the provisions of the Wetlands Management (Ramsar Sites) Regulation,[168] is woefully inadequate to serve it purpose of conserving and managing Wetlands. For example it imposes an amount of not more than C[169]100, 000 (this is a little over $10[170]) and not less than C50, 000 and /or imprisonment on first time offenders and, in case of continuing offence, an amount of not more than C50, 000 in respect of each day that the offence continues.[171] The absence of implementing legislation for the various treaties ratified by Ghana has contributed to the dearth of judicial decisions on environmental law by the Ghanaian courts. There are barely any reported decisions based on legislation enacted pursuant to any of the ratified conventions on the environment. It has been proposed that in the absence of some environmental legislation, the fundamental human rights provisions of the 1992 Constitution, could serve as a basis for the recognition and enforcement of environmental norms in the light of similar practices elsewhere.[172]

The economic situation in Ghana is a contributing factor to ineffective implementation of international environmental law. Most obviously, enforcement is affected by the

---

[167] MARPOL, supra note 99. See rules on discharge and equipment standards
[168] Ramsar Regulation, supra note 93
[169] Ghanaian Cedi
[170] $1 is equivalent to C870
[171] Ramsar Regulation, supra ss. 8
[172] Sarpong, supra note 165 at 18 (where recommends practices of Latin American countries and India who recognize the right to a healthy environment through the right to life, property, privacy and culture. He cites the Columbian case of Fundepublico v. Mayor of Bugalagrande where the constitutional court noted that, "the right to a healthy environment is conceived as a group of basic conditions surrounding man and

relationship between the cost of implementation and the wealth of country. Developed countries who have relatively high growth rates are always able and willing to comply with their environmental obligations no matter how costly than poorer countries who are experiencing slow economic growth. On the other hand, if the cost of implementation is very low, or if implementation produces a net economic gain, a country's level of economic well-being is not very critical for implementation because the decisive factor is the relationship between the cost of implementation and the capacity of a country's economy to absorb them. Ghana like most developing countries find it extremely difficult to afford the cost of implementing most of their obligations under these treaties because the cost is too high and they simply cannot absorb these costs especially if financial assistance is not available. Ghana like most African countries gives priority to economic growth at the expense of environmental quality. They view international environmental conventions, which seek to regulate use of natural resources for the common concern of mankind as a kind of interference with their permanent sovereignty over natural resources. In view of this, there is very little or no will or commitment to enact into domestic legislation international environmental conventions whiles, every effort is being made to attract Foreign Direct Investment (FDI) from Transnational Corporations who are drawn into developing countries because of unlimited access to natural resources, cheap labor and lax environmental laws.[173]

---

which define his life as a member of the community and allow his biological and individual survival, in addition to his normal participation and integral development in the society")
[173] Hunter, supra note 13 at 1437

The Ministry of Science and Environment charged with the responsibility of formulating proposals for legislation on the environment based on studies and research lack readily available information systems to effectively operate. The EPA charged with the enormous task of regulating the environment and ensuring implementation of government policies relating to the environment is poorly equipped in terms of both personnel and funding. Grants from the government and other donor agencies to the Trust Fund are woefully inadequate to enable it to effectively carry out its mandate of enforcing environmental regulation in the country. Those charged with the task of enforcing the regulations are either poorly equipped to discharge their duties or are ignorant of the provisions they are enforcing. There is therefore the need to upgrade administrative capacity of the institutions tasked with enforcing environmental regulations like the EPA. The EPA has not been able to carry out its proposed integrated environmental planning and management system, due to these and many other problems.[174] Ghana's Decentralization policies to promote public participation at the grass root level in environmental decision-making has not been effective due to lack of incentive to induce participation.

---

[174] *For instance the EPA has not been able implement its policy of polluter pays principle due to the low income levels of the majority of the population, especially those in the rural areas. The use of economic and financial instruments like product charges, pollution charges, user charges have been very difficult to implement.*

Inadequate funding by donor agencies has also contributed to the paucity of domestic legislation to implement international environmental conventions. It was agreed at the Rio Conference[175] that in order to facilitate the implementation of Agenda 21, developed countries would assist African countries in particular with the appropriate technologies and funding on affordable terms. Limited success has been achieved in this area so far for Ghana. Even though Ghana has received external assistance, they have been inadequate and procedural difficulties make it very difficult to access the little funding that is available.[176] Incremental funding, which is easily accessible and largely in the form of grants rather than loans will still be needed to continue the implementation of Agenda 21. Other policy gaps that impede the effectiveness of implementation in Ghana are inadequate incentives to encourage conformity and compliance with environmental regulations. Standard gaps in environmental research and inadequate mechanisms to encourage the flow of information is also a huge problem.

---

[175] *Rio Declaration, supra note 2*

[176] *In spite of the above situation, external aid represents a significant share of national budgets in Africa especially in sub-Saharan Africa. Dependence on external aid raises concerns in Africa as to the adequacy of funds, sustainability of interventions, and freedom to reflect national policies rather than priorities of the donors.*

CHAPTER V: RECOMMENDATION

The above discussion has shown that for Multilateral Environmental Agreements to have the force and effect they have to be enacted into legislation and adequate policy framework for environmental management should be in place. Ghana to some extent has existing constitutional, institutional and legislative framework to undertake its commitments under the various Multilateral Environmental Agreements it has ratified. Although Ghana has made improvements in its environmental management, many challenges still need to be address. What it needs is to enact legislations, that will be in consonance with its treaty obligations, address constitutional and policy gaps in the existing environmental policy by reviewing and recommending actions that can be achieved and get the needed funding to implement its environmental policies. It must also address environmental problems directly by tackling the problems of land degradation, deforestation, loss of biodiversity, pollution and dumping of hazardous waste to improve its prospects for sustainable development. Finally, Ghana must also address the issue of poverty, which is the main cause of environmental degradation.

Not long ago, Ghana and many other African countries had limited laws and institutional arrangements for environmental management, and therefore could not adequately address environmental problems.[177] The NEAP processes adopted has allowed Ghana to formulate relevant environmental policies, to enact new laws and has served as a guideline to review sectoral policies and its laws.

---
[177] Boon, supra note 11 at 32

Even though these policies, laws and regulation seems enough to serve as a good basis for sound environmental management, more could be done and need to be done, although more laws and institutions does not necessarily guarantee better environmental management. However the fact that Ghana's environment continues to deteriorate at an alarming rate indicates low level of implementation and enforcement. The sectoral approach to environmental management sometimes results in inconsistencies in the laws, and other problems like inadequate human resources and finances largely hinder effective implementation. Although Ghana has improved its policy frame-work for more effective environmental management, there is a need for more. The following recommendations have been proposed:

It must be noted that, the responsibility of implementing these recommendations lies with the government, which may seek assistance from other sources like the African Ministerial Conference on Environment (AMCEN) and other international organization to accelerate implementation.[178]

The government must promote cross-cutting action. Cross-cutting actions are wide in scope and involves promoting increased regional and sub regional cooperation on environmental issues, enhancing institutional capacity, addressing policy failures, promoting good governance, mobilizing domestic financial resources, enforcing compliance, setting targets and monitoring performance and NGO involvement.[179] African governments and Ghana in particular should seek partnership with the international community, to support regional and sub regional institutions such as the ECOWAS and SADC.

---

[178] See Global Environment Outlook 2000, available at: www.unep.org/geo2000/english/0147.htm
[179] See Africa Environment Outlook: Past, Present and Future Perspectives available at: Http://www.unep.org.aeo/330.htm

This will enable these institutions to provide technical support and assistance to African government in formulating programs of action to support the management of transboundary environmental resources and to formalize MEAs to effectively address issues like CITES and hazardous waste management.

The government should address policy failures. Ghana after Rio introduced many macroeconomics,[180] social, environmental and sectoral policies and enacted laws to achieve sustainable development and indeed environmental management has improved. However, some of these policies and laws have not been effective to address environmental problems. There is the need to review some of these laws and policies, remove the contradictions, and address the main causes of failures. Capacity for policy analysis must be created to analyze policies and ensure early detection of failures in implementation. This will work better if there is greater will and commitment to the implementation of the policies and laws that has been adopted. Ghana must emulate South Africa, whose constitution confers on every citizen the right to an environment that is not harmful to health or well-being. The right to have the environment protected for the benefit of the present and future generations through reasonable legislative and other measures that: (i) prevent pollution and ecological degradation (ii) promote conservation; and (iii) secure ecological sustainable development and use of natural resources while promoting justifiable economic and social development.[181] Such a provision will ensure the governments commitment to environmental policies and the courts will readily enforce it against the government of the day. Any proposed legislation must also reflect the principles and obligations of the Multilateral Environmental Agreements on the subject.

---

[180] *Boon, supra note 11 at 34*
[181] *See S. Afr. Const. art. 86-87*

The government must improve environmental education and awareness. Ghana in its Environmental Action plan proposed environmental studies at both the first and second cycle education level. More efforts must be put into promoting environmental education. The government must invest in the formulation and implementation of formal and informal education strategies. Broad participation by the public in decision-making is an important element of Agenda 21 of Rio because, combined with greater accountability, it is basic to the concept of sustainable development. For the public to effectively participate, they must be aware of the environmental problems, and Agenda 21 recognizes that there is lack of awareness of the correlation between human activities and the environment due to inadequate information. Even though, Ghana through its decentralization policy has invested significantly in this area, this effort needs to be sustained at the local level.[182]

The role of NGOs cannot be under estimated.[183] Even though some NGOs have been effective in lobbying and advocating environmental quality, most of them operating in Ghana are relatively weak in both technical and institutional aspect of projects planning and implementation. Ghana should encourage ENGOs by supporting their efforts in environmental management.

One of the major problems facing the EPA in Ghana is inadequate environmental data and information. Ghana needs to improve environmental information systems as a basis for sound decision-making. AMCEN and other international bodies should support Ghana and other African countries to create databases to enhance networking and

---

[182] *Boon, supra 11 at 34*
[183] *Id.*

collaboration between Ghana and other African states. This will allow countries within the Region to exchange and share experiences on implementation.

Although, Ghana has various laws and regulations governing environmental management, their enforcement is generally weak. The EPA, which is the main enforcement body on environment, is saddled with many challenges, they lack the administrative capacity needed to effectively enforce environmental laws and regulations. To enforce environmental laws adequately, the regulatory authority must be able to monitor compliance and two factors affect this ability.[184] First, the EPA as a regulatory body needs adequate feedback mechanism. These can assume different forms, including on-site monitoring by inspectors, reporting requirements, the use of complaint mechanisms and a close working relationship with NGOs. Secondly, the effectiveness of these mechanisms depends on how well the government is able to regulate the activities of the potential violators. There is a need to build capacity in the form of finance; data and personnel to adequately enforce existing legislation and to better appreciate their roles. Economic instrument linked with the system of taxation should be used as an incentive to encourage desirable behavior.

Ghana must also address the issue of poverty since poverty has been one of the major causes of environmental degradation in the country. High rate of poverty has made it very difficult to implement and enforce environmental regulations and certain principles in Ghana, like the polluter pays principle. Even though there is no uniform solution to poverty, it is imperative for Ghana to adopt poverty reduction strategies. To do this Ghana needs to endorse and promote principles of sustainable development; increase industrial development necessary to provide employment and to increase resources to *promote economic growth as well. Industrialization should focus on the agricultural sector and it should be geared towards adding value to export products. A caveat in this regard is to promote environmentally sustainable industrialization, which will not further speed up environmental degradation. Developed countries on the other hand must open up their markets and eliminate all subsidies on export products competing with them. There is also the need to promote access to health care and improve infrastructure and human settlement to reduce congestion and pollution in the urban areas. There is also the need to identify scientific and technological loopholes relating to environmental management and to address the gaps by accessing indigenous and external technologies to enhance environmental management.*

Ghana needs external support if it is to succeed in effectively implementing its environmental obligations and to reverse the current trend in environmental degradation. Ghana even though a poor and heavily indebted country, still needs increased financial resources from the World Bank, and to improve on its operational and project implementation procedures of the GEF.[185]

The environment serves as the basis for human health; well-being, security, and majority of Ghanaian rural dwellers depend on the natural resources of the environment for their livelihood. There is the need to halt and reverse the current trend in environmental degradation by directly addressing the problems. For instance legislation and regulations on UNCLOS should be reviewed, legislation on CCD should be enacted and be implemented in a timely and effective manner by training and adequately equipping personnel, including traditional authorities in the prevention and regulation of bush fires,

---

[184] Weiss, supra note151 at 31
[185] Africa Environment Outlook, supra note 179

adopting viable and sound land use policies and plans.[186] Legislation is also needed to implement the Montreal Protocol, the CBD, MARPOL and the Bamako Convention on Hazardous waste and funds must be obtain to put in place projects for effective waste management of non hazardous waste.

Where there has been extensive poaching in wildlife protected areas, national effort is required to rehabilitate these areas through species reintroduction and habitat restoration projects. Ex situ conservation of rare, vulnerable and endangered species should be promoted. Ghana must in addition enter into partnership with other countries to support the management of chemical products, in accordance with chapter 19 of Agenda 21 and other conventions. Finally, any proposed legislation must incorporate the various environmental principles to serve as guidelines against which the conduct of the state, individual and corporations can be measure.[187] So far Ghana does not have any environmental legislation which has these principles[188] embodied in it.

---

[186] *Sarpong, supra* note 30 at 27
[187] *Id.* at 34
[188] *These principles even though are not binding have significant impact on international environmental policy as they provide framework for the development and conservation of national environmental laws. They include the principle of state sovereignty, sustainable development, duty to implement effective environmental legislation, polluter and user pays principle, preventive principles, access to information, duty to access environmental impacts, public participation, precautionary principle and the principle of international co-operation.*

CHAPTER VI   CONCLUSION

It must be noted that, in spite of the low economic and technological growth, Ghana and African countries in general have adopted quite a positive attitude towards the environment and their duty to implement effective environmental legislation. However, much more needs to be done in this area. It is one thing to ratify an environmental convention and another to implement legislation to give effect to them. Sometimes merely enacting legislations have not adequately solve the environmental problem for which it was made however, it is a step in the right direction because it will open avenues to address policy failures and know how to act in the future. African countries should back ratification by effective environmental legislation to give them binding effect and allow the courts to enforce them. By enacting effective legislation, African countries will not only be complying with their duty under international law but these law will also serve as yard stick by which the conduct of government and individual will be measured. It is commendable to note that at least 35 countries in Africa have constitutional provisions ensuring a right to a healthy environment. This means African countries have realized the value of constitutional provisions as a strong tool to protect the environment.[189] The Ghanaian Constitution[190] must be amended to guarantee the right to a healthy environment as South Africa and many countries[191] have done. In this way it can be enforced against the government alternatively, the courts should be encouraged to broadly interpret the right to life embodied in the Constitution to include the right to a healthy environment as is done in the Latin American countries.

---

[189] Carl Bruch & Wole Coker *Breathing Life into Fundamental Principles: Constitutional Environmental Law in Africa*, innovation, vol. 6, no. 2, p.1 (1999)
[190] Ghana Const. supra 154

On the other hand, developed countries should readily assist African countries to implement their commitments under international environmental law. Many projects have been proposed, but they have either been given up or ignored because of unavailability of funds to effectively Implement them. While appealing to developed countries to provide financial and technological resources, African countries should exhibit greater will and commitment to environmental management giving environmental management a higher priority and allocate adequate funds to carry into effect proposed legislations and projects.

I hope the Ghanaian government will adopt some of these recommendations.

---

[191] See The People's Republic of China, Art 26 that provides that the state must protect and improve the environment in which the people live. It must prevent and control pollution and other public hazards.

BIBLIOGRAPHY

PRIMARY SOURCES:

Constitutions

Ghana (GH) Constitution

South Africa (S. AFR) Constitution art.86-87

Legislation

Concession Act, 1962 (Act 124)

Control and Prevention of Bush fires Law, 1990, (PNDCL 229)

Economic Plant Protection Decree, 1979, (AFRCD 47)

Environmental Protection Act, 1994, (Act 490)

Environmental Assessment Regulation, 1999, LI 1652

Environmental Assessment (Amendment) Regulation, 2002, LI 1703 Fisheries Commission Act, 1993, (Act 457)

Fisheries Law, 1991, (PNDCL 256)

Forestry Ordinance, 1927, CAP 157

Forest Protection (Amendment) Law, 1986 (PNDCL142)

Maritime Zones (Delimitation) Law, 1986, (PNDCL 159)

Timber Resource Management Act, (Act 547) (citation incomplete)

Wetland Management (Ramsar Site) Regulation 1999 LI 1659

Wild Animals Preservation Act, 1961, (Act 43)

Wild Reserve Regulations LIs 685 and 710 as amended by LIs 1283 and1284

SECONDAY SOURCES:

International Conventions and Treaties

African Convention on the Conservation of Nature and Natural Resources September 15, 1968 1001 U.N.T.S. 3

Bamako Convention on the Ban of the Import into Africa and the Control of Transboundary Movement and Management of Hazardous Wastes within Africa 30 ILM 773 (1991)

Basel Convention on the Control of Transboundary Movement of Hazardous Wastes and their Disposal March 22, 1989, 28 ILM 657 (1989)

Convention on Biological Diversity

Convention on the Conservation of Migratory Species of Wild Animals 19 ILM 15 1980

Convention on International Trade in Endangered species of Fauna and Flora 27 U.S.T. 1087, 12 ILM 1085 (1973)

Convention on the Protection of the World Cultural and Natural Heritage 27 U.S.T. 37, 11 ILM 1358 (1972)

Convention on Wetlands of International Importance especially as Waterfowl Habitat (1971) (Ramsar Convention) 11 ILM 963 1972)

International Tropical Timber Agreement

London Convention for the Prevention of Pollution from Ships (MARPOL) 12 ILM 1319 (1973)

Montreal Protocol on Substance that Deplete the Ozone Layer 26 ILM 1550 (1987)

Rio Declaration on Environment and Development of United Nations Conference on Environment and Development 1992 31 ILM 874 (1992)

Stockholm Declaration on Human Environment of United Nations Conference on Human Environment, June 16, 1972, 11 ILM 1416 (1972)

United Nations Convention on the Law of the Sea 21 ILM 1261 (1982)

United Nations Convention on Climate Change

United Nations Convention to Combat Desertification June 17, 1994, 331 ILM1328

Vienna Convention for the Protection of the Ozone Layer March 22, 1985, 26 ILM 1529 (1987)

Vienna Convention on the Law of Treaties

Law Review Articles

Carl Bruch & Wole Coker Breathing Life into Fundamental Principles: Constitutional Environmental Law in Africa, Innovation, vol. 6, no. 2 (1999)

George Sarpong, "From Stockholm to Rio; some Ghanaian Responses to the problems of the Environment, 19 UGLJ (1993-1995)

George Sarpong Domestication of Biodiversity Conservation Instrument in Ghana (2000) (Unpublished Report)

George Sarpong, Ghana Fisheries Legislation: the Ajax Case and UNCLOS, RGL 17 (1989-1990)

Kotey "Land and Tree and Rural Development Forestry in Northern Ghana" 19 UGLJ (1993-1995)

Luc Hens & Emmanuel Boon, Legal and Economic Environmental Policy in Ghana, Vrije University Brussels, Belgium (2000)

Ronald Mitchell "Regime Design Matters: Intentional Oil Pollution and Treaty Compliance" Int. Org. 425, 426, 428 (1994)

Cases:

The Ajax Case no. 85/89 March 1989, National Public Tribunal, Accra

The Chorzow Factory Case P.C.I.J., Ser. A, No, 17

Books:

David Hunter et al., International Environmental Law and Policy (4th ed 2002)

David Victor et al., The Implementation and Effectiveness of International Environmental Commitments: Theory and Practice (1998)

Edith Brown Weiss & Harold Jacobson, Engaging Countries: Strengthening Compliance with International Environmental Accords (1998)

Lori F. Damrosch et al., International Law (4th ed.2001)

INTERNET SOURCES:

Africa Environmental Outlook; past present and future perspectives available at:
http://www.unep.org.aeo

Emmanuel Boon (2000) Legal and Economic Environmental policy in Ghana available at: http://www.vub.ac.be/MEKO/publications/epghana.doc

Ghana environmental Profile available at www.un.org/esa/agenda21/natlinfo//contr.ghana/inst.htm

Ghana Action Plan vol. 1 available at http://www.wri.org/wdcess/gh88_640.html

Ghana Environmental Protection Agency http://www.epa.gov.gh/

Global Environmental Outlook (2000) available at:
http://www.unep.org/geo2000/english/0146.htm

Handbook on implementation of Conventions to Biological Diversity in Africa available at: http:// www.unep.org/padelia/publications/handbook

JICA country Profile available at:

http://www.jica.go.jp/English/global/env/profiles/e99gha.pdf

i want morebooks!

Buy your books fast and straightforward online - at one of world's fastest growing online book stores! Free-of-charge shipping and environmentally sound due to Print-on-Demand technologies.

Buy your books online at
www.get-morebooks.com

Kaufen Sie Ihre Bücher schnell und unkompliziert online – auf einer der am schnellsten wachsenden Buchhandelsplattformen weltweit! Versandkostenfrei und dank Print-On-Demand umwelt- und ressourcenschonend produziert.

Bücher schneller online kaufen
www.morebooks.de

 VDM Verlagsservicegesellschaft mbH
Dudweiler Landstr. 99 Telefon: +49 681 3720 174 info@vdm-vsg.de
D - 66123 Saarbrücken Telefax: +49 681 3720 1749 www.vdm-vsg.de

Lightning Source UK Ltd.
Milton Keynes UK
UKHW012350210421
382415UK00001B/67